DREAMING
AND THINKING

Dreaming and Thinking is one of a series of low-cost books under the title **PSYCHOANALYTIC ideas** which brings together the best of Public Lectures and other writings given by analysts of the British Psycho-Analytic Society on important psychoanalytic subjects.

Other titles in the Psychoanalytic ideas series:

Child Analysis Today
Luis Rodriguez De la Sierra (editor)

Shame and Jealousy: The Hidden Turmoils
Phil Mollon

Spilt Milk: Perinatal Loss and Breakdown
Joan Raphael-Leff (editor)

Unconscious Phantasy
Riccardo Steiner (editor)

Psychosis (Madness)
Paul Williams (editor)

Adolescence
Inge Wise (editor)

Psychoanalytic Ideas and Shakespeare
Inge Wise and Maggie Mills (editors)

DREAMING
AND THINKING

Editor

Rosine Jozef Perelberg

Series Editors

Inge Wise and *Paul Williams*

Routledge
Taylor & Francis Group

LONDON AND NEW YORK

First published 2000 by the Institute of Psycho-Analysis, London

Published 2006 by Karnac Books Ltd.

Published 2018 by Routledge
2 Park Square, Milton Park, Abingdon, Oxon OX14 4RN
52 Vanderbilt Avenue, New York, NY 10017

Routledge is an imprint of the Taylor & Francis Group, an informa business

British Library Cataloguing in Publication Data

A C.I.P. for this book is available from the British Library

ISBN-13: 978-1-85575-978-7 (pbk)

Edited, designed, and produced by The Studio Publishing Services Ltd,
Exeter EX4 8JN

To Daniel

CONTENTS

ACKNOWLEDGEMENTS

This book is derived from a "Day of Public Lecture on *Dreaming and Thinking*" I organized on the 21st June 1997, from which the papers by Ignêz Sodré and Peter Fonagy, as well as aspects of my "Introduction" have been retained.

I am grateful to all the authors of this book, especially those who finished their chapters some time ago, for their support for this project, and for maintaining their faith that this book would eventually come to light.

To Inge Wise, the series editor, and Paul Williams, for their support and enthusiasm.

To all my students and colleagues, who over the years have attended my seminars. To the candidates of the Institute of Psycho-Analysis who attended my Freud Seminars, over the years, and to my students at the Msc in Psychoanalytic Theory at UCL. To the groups I have taught in recent years from Stuttgart, Heidelberg, Berlin, and Frankfurt for their receptivity to my ideas. I would especially like to thank my colleagues at the BAP who attended the course in 1996, for members which I entitled, "Dreaming, thinking, fantasying", where many of the ideas of my own paper were first discussed and tested out.

To my patients, who are consistently my main source of reflection and inspiration.

To Jill Duncan, for doing the impossible, and always finding for me the references I needed, even in the middle of the Institute of Psycho-Analysis move to Byron House.

To Judith Perle, for her literary knowledge and unwavering support.

To my family and friends, for their consistent presence.

Finally, I would like also to thank so many of my colleagues at the British Society for an environment where differences coexist and are continually discussed, at times with great passion.

I would like to thank *The International Journal of Psychoanalysis* for permission to reproduce Victor Sedlak's paper "The dream space and counter-transference".

I would like to thank Karnac for permission to publish a revised version of Gregorio Kohon's chapter, "Dreams, acting out and symbolic impoverishment", from *No Lost Certainties to be Recovered* (London: Karnac, 1999).

CONTRIBUTORS

Sara Flanders, PhD, is training analyst and supervisor of the British Psychoanalytical Society, and is on the staff of the Brent Adolescent Centre. She is also in private practice. She is the editor of *The Dream Discourse Today, Volume 17* in The New Library of Psychoanalysis.

Peter Fonagy, PhD, is training and supervising analyst at the British Psychoanalytical Society. He is Freud Memorial Professor of Psychoanalysis and director of the sub-department of Clinical Health Psychology at University College London. He is also Director of Research at the Anna Freud Centre, London. As well as being the author of numerous papers in several international journals, he has edited *What Works for Whom: A Critical Review of Psychotherapy Research* (1996) and *Psychoanalysis on the Move: The Work of Joseph Sandler* (1999). He is the author of *Attachment Theory and Psychoanalysis* (2001).

Gregorio Kohon is a training analyst and supervisor of the British Psychoanalytical Society. In 1988 he co-founded, with Valli Shaio Kohon, the Brisbane Centre for Psychoanalytic Studies, which he directed until 1994. He works in London in private practice and is the editor of *The British School of Psychoanalysis—The Independent Tradition* (1986), *The Dead Mother—The Work of Andre Green* (1999), New Library of Psychoanalysis, and author of *No Lost Certainties to be Recovered*.

Rosine Jozef Perelberg, PhD, is a training analyst and supervisor of the British Psychoanalytical Society. She trained in Social Anthropology at the Federal University of Rio de Janeiro and gained her PhD from the London School of Economics, London University. She co-edited, with Ann Miller, *Gender and Power in Families* (1990); with Joan Raphael-Leff *Female Experience: Three Generations of British Analyst Work with Women* (1997); and has also edited *Psychoanalytic Understanding of Violence and Suicide* (1999). She has taught widely and published numerous articles, both in England and abroad. She works in private practice in London.

Victor Sedlak, PhD, is a training analyst and supervisor at the British Psychoanalytic Society. He was a clinical psychologist before training as a psychotherapist at the Tavistock Clinic and then going on to do psychoanalytic training. He is in private psychoanalytic practice in the North of England. His research interests include psychoanalytic supervision, dreams and the psychoanalytic process.

Ignês Sodré is a training analyst and supervisor of the British Psychoanalytical Society. Originally she trained as clinical psychologist in Rio de Janeiro, before completing her training in the British Society. She teaches candidates of the British Society and abroad. She has published *Imagining Characters* with A. S. Byatt, as well as various papers in international journals on clinical practice and literature.

Introduction

Rosine Jozef Perelberg

The publication of Freud's *The Interpretation of Dreams* (1900) could be said to mark the birth of psychoanalysis, as dreams became paradigmatic of the unconscious (Green, 1986, 2000). It is not surprising, therefore, that dream interpretation, as it is practised currently in the British Psycho-Analytical Society, bears the mark of the modern advances and discoveries in the field of psychoanalysis itself.

This present book contains some modern contributions to the understanding and interpretation of dreams developed by contemporary psychoanalysts in the British Society. At its core is an exploration of the connections between dreaming and thinking, and the way in which dreams may provide the analysts' best clues to their patients' states of mind. The varied contributions to this volume further extend the perception that the interpretation of dreams allows access to a theory of mind, to the ways in which analysands conceive their experiences of their inner world of thoughts and feelings. It is crucial for the analyst, during a session, to differentiate, conceptually and clinically, between different types of mental processes. An understanding of the type of constructs presented by patients—i.e. the quality, content or function of their dreams, daydreams thoughts or actions—at each moment in an analytic session represents an important means of identifying the structure of their psychic states. Each author crucially links dreams to the transference, so facilitating a deeper understanding of the analytic process itself. The ten patients who are discussed in this book bring to their analysts their innermost primitive and distressed feelings, and seek their help.

In 1993, Flanders edited an excellent book, *The Dream Discourse Today*, which contained some of the seminal papers on dreams published in the 1960s, 1970s, and the early 1980s in Europe and America. The present book may be seen as complementary to that volume, with papers written in the last five years by Members of the British Society.

Freud and the discovery of the unconscious

Freud stated, in his "New Introductory Lectures" (1932, p. 7), that it was with the discovery of the laws that govern the formation of dreams that psychoanalysis moved, "from being a psychotherapeutic procedure to being a depth psychology". In *The Interpretation of Dreams*, published in 1900, he described what he believed to be the origins of the unconscious, the rules which govern its operation, and its imperious impulse towards expression in consciousness. We are only able to access the contents of the unconscious mind via its representations in consciousness: in the dreams we remember, for example, or slips of the tongue, or in symptoms, such as phobias and anxieties. Through his study of his own dreams and free associations, and those of his patients, Freud began to understand that the contents of the unconscious were organized differently from conscious thoughts. He termed the rules governing the unconscious, "primary process". Unconscious thoughts must undergo a process of transformation or distortion before they are accessible to consciousness. Primary process concerns the rules or grammar of that transformation. These rules disguise unacceptable or traumatic unconscious ideas, which can only be understood via a process of interpretation.

Freud indicated four fundamental rules that guide dream work. The first of these rules is displacement. This allows an apparently insignificant idea or object to be invested with great intensity, which originally belonged elsewhere. This displacement takes place because consciousness finds the original object of these intense feelings—such as aggression, hate or sexual longing towards a parent—unacceptable. These thoughts therefore undergo repression and appear in a disguised form. Displacement corresponds to metonymy, which establishes a connection between words whose relationship both in terms of form and content are not obvious, so binding together incongruous phantasies.

Another rule of primary process is condensation. This is the means by which, according to Freud, thoughts which are mutually contradictory make no attempt to do away with each other, but persist side by side. They often combine to form condensations, just as though there were no contradictions between them, or arrive at compromises, which our conscious thoughts would never tolerate. Condensation is another way in which unacceptable thoughts pushing through into consciousness are disguised. This also accounts for the fact that the manifest content of dreams is generally smaller than the latent contents. This mechanism of condensation can be seen in terms of what linguists see as metaphor.

Another aspect of the dream work is what Freud addresses as conditions of representability, whereby dreams represent words in figurative form, in images. Freud thought this was the most interesting aspect of dream work. An example is the representation of an important person by someone who is "high up", at the top of a tower. Words in dreams can be thing-representations, representations of things.

All dreams are subject to secondary revision, which is an attempt by the dreamer to organize, revise, and establish connections in the dream to make its account intelligible. "This function behaves in the manner that the poet maliciously ascribes to philosophers; it fills up the gaps in the dream-structure with shreds bad patches' (Freud, 1900, p. 490).

Freud's distinction between the manifest and the latent content of dreams is important. The work that transforms latent thoughts into manifest dream content is called dream work (condensation, displacement, secondary revision, and considerations of representability). The work that operates in the opposite direction, that seeks to move from the manifest content to the latent thoughts, is the work of interpreting the dream. The manifest content is what the dreamer remembers. The latent content is what gives the dream its meaning, the dream thoughts reached through the interpretation of the dream. The process of interpretation allows access to the wish expressed in the dream, which takes the shape of a hallucinatory wish fulfilment. The dream itself does not think, but presents an action inside the dream. The immediate material that gives content to the dream is usually something from the day before—a day residue—which must nevertheless, according to Freud, be linked to an infantile wish in order to give rise to a dream. In this model, desire itself becomes the main source of functioning for the unconscious. In his interpretation of dreams, Freud searched for a normal thought, repressed and transformed by the work of primary process (Mannoni, 1968, p. 71).

Freud compared the process of dream interpretation to a rebus or picture puzzle, made up of a mixture of pictographic, phonetic, and ideogrammatic elements, each of which requires a different process of translation. This, in itself, points to the radical heterogeneity of the unconscious. By replacing each element with a syllable or word one can arrive at a sense of the whole. What each dream element signifies is often revealed through the dreamer's free associations to that element, although one should also remember that Freud postulated that in every dream there is a navel that is, by definition, inaccessible. "There is at least one spot in every dream at which it is unplumbable—a navel, as it were, that is its point of contact with the unknown" (Freud, 1900, p. 111).

Free association, where a patient is encouraged to say the first thing that comes into his or her mind, allows for unconscious processes to be expressed. A person can never predict where these free associations will lead. Even if the meaning of a dream appears to be clear, it is the network of associations that expands or reveals that which has been disguised. This is reached by a process of inference and construction.

It is important to note that, although one tends to think that dreams in analysis may have the analyst in mind, Freud suggests that part of the dream is not susceptible to external influences: "On the mechanism of dream formation itself, on the dream-work in the strict sense of the word, one never exercises any influence: of that one may be quite sure" (Freud, 1923, p. 114).

In 1914, Freud wrote a completely new section to *The Interpretation of Dreams* which was devoted to symbols. From then onwards he maintained a tension between two positions in connection with symbolism, which he viewed as another important expression of the primary process. On the one hand, he highlighted the universality of that which could be symbolized, which could be found not only in the same individual, and between individuals, but also in myth, religion, and folklore across cultures. On the other hand, he insisted on the crucial importance of the patient's specific associations, which were necessary to achieve an understanding of the meaning of a particular symbol for that patient. He suggested that there are limited numbers of "things" which find expression in symbols: the human body, parents, children, brothers and sisters, birth, death, nakedness, and sexual life. For example, an emperor and empress in a dream, or a king and queen, usually symbolize the parents; rooms symbolize women, their entrances and exits the openings of the body. Sharp weapons, or long and stiff objects, symbolize the penis; cupboards, boxes, carriages, and ovens may symbolize the womb. Other symbols are less obvious. A staircase, for instance, may symbolize sexual intercourse, because it contains the idea of "upstairs" to the bedrooms, and "going up" inside a house, and imply effort and rhythmic movement, or an erection.

These universal symbols are not freshly made, so to speak, by each individual. It is as if they lie in the mind, complete and ready for use. Because these symbols are the same in all people, when they are employed as images by novelists and poets, they can communicate additional layers of meaning with great power and resonance.

Dreams both reveal and conceal concern with primary issues. In Greek etymology, a symbol consisted of two halves of a broken object that could be fitted together. It is the link that creates meaning, a notion which implies that meaning was there at the outset. The psychoanalyst usually tries to integrate these two aspects of symbolism, the universal and the particular. For instance, one knows that houses tend to represent the body, the mind, or the mother's body. In one of the clinical examples discussed in my own chapter in this volume, I describe a patient, an artist, who had the following dream at the beginning of his analysis.

There was a beautiful house, the most beautiful house one could imagine, surrounded by lush gardens, and filled with works of art and famous paintings. It was very spacious, one room leading to another. There was glass surrounding it, however, and one was not able to penetrate it. One had to admire it from the outside.

It was in the process of associations with this dream that we had access to several layers of meaning, such as the experience that there was no live communication between inside and outside, between his inner world and the external one. Everything was either locked in or out. This was a dream we repeatedly came back to throughout our work together. The house also represented the body of a mother whom he experienced as ungiving and impenetrable. Finally, it represented his fears that whatever he produced would be trapped inside her.

The unconscious is also characterized by the absence of negation: "no" does not exist. So a statement which appears in its negative form might actually imply its opposite. The statement, "this dream is not about my mother", might actually indicate that the dream is about the patient's mother. It is the network of associations which reveals who the characters depicted in the dream represent.

Another characteristic of primary process is the absence of chronological time. Timelessness characterizes the unconscious mode of functioning. Different times coexist, and this is what allows one to dream that one is a child, a baby or an older person, all at the same time.

In his paper written in 1915, "The Unconscious", Freud (1917a) put forward his thesis that the unconscious is present in the gaps between the observable. It is characterized by its radical discontinuity in relation to consciousness. The psychoanalytic domain is the domain of that which is, in fact, not accessible to observations, but can only be reached through its derivatives. Thus, it is easier to say what it is not than what it is: an absence of negation, of a sense of time, characterized by thing presentation, symbolism, and metaphors. The theme of the radical discontinuity of the unconscious in relation to what is accessible, remained a constant in Freud's formulations and continued through his reformulation into the structural model of the mind. Freud felt that dreams provided convincing evidence of psychic life, more so than conscious activity, which was unreliable because of processes of rationalization.

Modern perspectives

Have our perspectives on the connections between dreaming and the mind changed since Freud's time? We now know, with later contributions from analysts in the British Society, that dreaming may reflect a capacity to create a specific mental space. From this perspective, dreaming is the result of a developmental process that takes place in a facilitation environment, which requires the presence of a mother who has the capacity to reflect on her baby's mental states. We also know, however, that at times dreams can be used defensively, so that psychoanalysts always pay attention to the form and function of dreams, rather than just their content. In his chapter, Gregorio Kohon points out how, at times, the telling of a dream itself may "be a form of acting out".

In the following pages, I will identify some of the main themes that underlie the chapters of this book.

1) Dream space: transitional space and mental space

Klein (1927) was the first to regard the play of a child as equivalent to free associations in an adult. Later, Sharpe (1937) established a connection between dreams and children's play, which she also related to the experience of the analytic session, a view developed by Lewin (1946, 1955), Khan (1962, 1974) and Stewart (1973).

Winnicott's work, on the function and development of play, was inspiring for the understanding of dreaming and its function in mental life and development. Winnicott pointed out the mother's facilitating function in enabling the child to have an illusion of omnipotence. Development takes place in the slow process of disillusionment that needs to be well modulated in the relationship with the mother. Winnicott (1971, p. 13) viewed potential space as, "The intermediate area ... that is allowed to infant between primary creativity and objective perception based on reality testing". It is, "unchallenged in respect of its belonging to inner or external reality, [it] constitutes the greater part of the infant's experience, and throughout life is retained in the intense experiencing that belongs to the arts, religion and imaginative living" (*ibid.*, p. 16). It is intermediate between the dream and the reality that is called cultural life (*ibid.*, p. 150). "In so far as the infant has not achieved transitional phenomena I think the acceptance of symbols is deficient, and the cultural life is poverty stricken" (Winnicott *et al.*, 1989, p. 57).

Another concept, that is relevant at this point, is that of mental space. *The Interpretation of Dreams* had already referred to a topographical model of the mind, using a spatial metaphor for Freud's mapping of the mind. Freud suggests in that work (p. 536) that, "the scene of action of dreams is different from that of waking life". He refers to the mind in terms of a "physical locality", although he is careful when he attempts to separate it from anatomical locality. Thoughts are, "never localised in organic elements of the nervous system but, as one might say, between them" (*ibid.*, p. 611).

Bion indicated the way in which the maternal function of containing thoughts and feelings is internalized and enables the creation of mental space. Using a mathematical metaphor, he pointed out that the geometrical concept of space derives from an experience of "the place where something was". If this concept is to be used to characterize mental phenomena, the concept of space, in dreams, designates the place where the lost object was, or the space where some form of emotion used to be (Bion, 1970, p. 10). It thus implies that an object's place has been lost. This mental space, as a thing in itself, is unknowable, although it can be represented by thoughts. Bion links the existence of this space to the experience of a container which is receptive to projections and thus allows for the realization of mental space, as well as the development of thought. According to Bion, thoughts lead to emotional development, and are to be contrasted with acting out, when the space left for thinking is felt to be intolerable and there is pressure for the apparent, immediate gratification that is felt to lie in action. As Hanna Segal (1980a, p. 101) suggested, "... only what can be adequately mourned can be adequately symbolized".

The absence of the object was also essential for Freud, as shown in his paper *Mourning and Melancholia* (1917b), which introduced a major shift in his work away from a theory that predominantly accounted for the vicissitudes of the drives, and toward a theory concerned with the internal world and identifications. Freud had already discussed the role of incorporation, whereby the individual would identify in the oral mode with the lost object; the constitution of the internal world was made through identifications. In *Beyond the Pleasure Principle* (1920), Freud interpreted his grandson's game with a cotton reel as the child's attempt at mastery of his mother's absence. In "Negation", her discussion of the same paper, Tonnesman (1992) stressed Freud's formulation that thinking begins "when the omnipotent control over the subjective object is shattered".

In the French psychoanalytic literature, the concept of desire is also related to an object that was known and then lost. Desire, thus, refers to an absence, and belongs to the same field as phantasy and dream (Mannoni, 1968, p. 111). I think that this may be linked to what Britton (1999, p. 117) has recently defined as "imagination": "This is the idea that the imagination as a place in the mind where unwitnessed events take place is in origin the phantasised primal scene". He calls this mental space "the other room", in which parental existence continues during parental absence. These thoughts introduce a relationship between a three-dimensional space and the oedipal situation.

These ideas are crucial to the issues discussed in the various chapters of this book. The dream space is identified with the capacity for mental space, which is ultimately connected to the capacity to bear the separation from the internal parents. The chapters that follow examine the vicissitudes that result when patients are unable to possess that space.

Ignês Sodré indicates how the story in a dream, the wishful phantasy, can be used as a model for the understanding of severely pathological manic defences against depressive affects, which are felt to be unbearable, Sodré examines one of Freud's own dreams, "Non vixit: a ghost story", which is about Freud's sense of guilt in relation to the death of his friend, Fleischl, in which the expression *non vivit* (he is not alive) was substituted by *non vixit* (he has not lived). Sodré uses this dream to formulate her thesis that unbearable events in the past are obliterated in a omnipotent way: "If he had not lived I could not have killed him". These ideas are then used in the understanding of the patient she discusses. She analyses a particular kind of manic defence against guilt, which is experienced as persecution, and suggests how this process finds expression in a dream (see also Byatt & Sodré 1995, p. 238).

Sara Flanders reflects on the relationship between the capacity to have a good dream and the good analytic hour, indicating how both involve the capacity for benign regression and for symbolization. Flanders discusses the analysis of a young female patient with an eating disorder, in order to illustrate her patient's difficulties in using the analytic space as symbolic space and her use of omnipotence defence. In the course of the analysis, Flanders indicates that the changes in the dreams produced by her patient parallel changes in the analysis.

Victor Sedlak's chapter vividly illustrates similarities between the conceptualization of the dream space and that of the analyst's function as a container of the patient's projections. He presents detailed clinical material from the analysis of two male patients, both of whom where unable to complete a dream about a particular emotional dilemma. Sedlak describes the way his patients created severe disturbance in the counter-transference and the analysts struggle to then work through this difficulty, with beneficial consequences for the patient.

Kohon's patient also expresses a failure to separate from his primary objects, which leaves him with an inability to mourn. He prematurely turns away from his objects in hatred. The absent object then becomes persecutory, a theme that finds an echo in Sarah Flander's and two of my own patients.

Peter Fonagy discusses his patient's difficulties in developing a reflective function, which leaves the patient limited in terms of his ability to imagine another person's behaviour in terms of mental state. Fonagy indicates that patients with severe personality disorders have difficulties in gaining access to their own mental experiences. Two clinical examples are discussed in his chapter. The first is a violent man who had to leave his previous therapist after a six-year therapy because of his threatening behaviour. The first dream in this analysis depicted the emptiness of Mr S's mind. The analyst's statements felt empty to the patient, like containers without content. In the second clinical example, Fonagy describes an aspect of the psychoanalytic treatment of Miss R, who was unable to accept the boundaries of the setting. The initial images in this patient's dreams revealed the lack of substance she experienced inside herself. In both cases, Fonagy also indicates the change in the quality of representation that can take place in the dreams of borderline patients in analysis.

With the three patients I discuss in my chapter, the issue of space, or lack of it, finds vivid illustration in their different initial dreams in analysis. Maria's initial dream contains a two-dimensional perspective, people who look like cartoon characters and have lost their three-dimensionality (or perhaps never had it?). In Michael's original dream, of a blank screen, it is a two-dimensional world that is being expressed, where thoughts and feelings are inchoate, unable to be represented. In Robert's first dream in his analysis, he is locked outside a house, outside the body of his mother, which cannot be explored, or locked out of his own mind. The chapter illustrates the changes in both the structure and content of their dreams that take place during these patients' analyses.

2) Dreams, acting out and the capacity to symbolize

The theme discussed above opens up the question of what happens when patients have difficulty in symbolizing (Segal, 1980a) or mentalizing (Fonagy & Target, 1995). Fonagy has pointed out that, if a characteristic of the human mind is the ability to relate to one's own as well as to others' mental states, some patients present a failure of this capacity, and they attempt to obliterate intolerable psychic experience. Following on from their work on the theory of mind, Fonagy and Target (1995) suggest that this problem can be traced back to a crucial state of development of the self, when the child searches in its primary objects for a representation of its own states of mind. When this is not successful, either because of inherent difficulties in the child or because of the care-givers inability, the child fails to build a coherent representation of its own mental states and those of others. Internal and external reality become confused with each other.

What happens in the treatment of these patients? Instead of symbolic expressions they reproduce archaic modes of relating to their internal objects, engaging the analyst in enactments in the consulting room. Their internal experiences are brought and lived in the transference. Insight is not derived from intellectualizations, but from felt experience (Sandler 1976, Joseph 1985, Feldman 1997). This is vividly illustrated in the account of Sodré's patient, who brought a "mindless" state of mind to her sessions; the past had to be consistently eliminated and, at the same time, had to be repeated concretely in the present.

Several of the patients described in this book operate, at times, in terms of what has been described as borderline or narcissistic states of mind, although they may express their destructiveness more clearly in the analytic process than in their relationship with the external world (see Kohon). Most of the patients express the way in which the boundaries of the setting itself are experienced as a threat.

In his chapter, Peter Fonagy indicates that the dreams of borderline patients have a special character. The primitive mechanical and inhuman imagery is often seen as reflecting the barrenness of their internal world. In his view, the dreams of these patients also contain a powerful residue from an early mode of self-reflection dating back to a phase of development when mental states are not yet appropriately represented, and when reflections have a concrete, rather than symbolic, quality. Fonagy depicts the quality of the dreams of borderline patients: "... the very bizarreness of their dreams, all point to the absence of mentalising elaboration as a consequence of partial failure of symbolisation". He emphasizes, however, that dreams should be regarded as reflections, albeit of a primitive kind. Fonagy discusses examples of dreams and their interpretation derived form two patients in analysis. He argues for the importance of dreams as a window into an identification of the patient's capacity to understand their own psychological state of being. He warns against the temptation to give meaning to material, "which as yet has little substance" and of over-interpreting dreams. Fonagy puts forward the idea that, "with borderline patients the elements of the dream are frequently far closer to the surface and far simpler in structure".

Kohon indicates how, in some patients, dreams are not there to be interpreted, "they are actions requiring a response, or the avoidance of a response ...", and:

> Dreams are used by the patient as instruments of intrigue, as a way to seduce or force the analyst to overlook something, or to divert his attention from something else happening in the session. Dreams, although symbolically created, become the equivalent of acting out ... [p. xx]

Flanders views her patient's bingeing as a temporary break-down of the patient's symbolic capacities, a failure in the capacity of the mind, "to bind symbolically the information coming from outside and inside". This failure may lead to a foreclosure of the mind. Flanders argues for the value of intense psychoanalytic treatment as the best treatment for such patients, in that the continuity embedded in the treatment allows for the disclosure of mental processes. The experience of the intensity of the psycho-analytic process helps the, "transformation of inchoate infantile experience through the work of maternal containment". At the end of her chapter anther dream indicates the patient's capacity to acquire a dream space.

In my chapter, I suggest that in the early stages of many analyses some patients' dreams are "predictive" of the future course of the analysis. These dreams contain a condensed narrative about the transference relationship and encapsulate a narrative that will unfold as the analysis progresses. They contain an announcement of an enactment that is already happening, or is about to take place. I further suggest that these dreams evoke a special feeling in the analyst, and provide images for an experience of the analysis for both patient and analyst that is still to be put into words. The analytic task is to change the course anticipated by these dreams, and introduce a difference in the "prediction" these dreams make.

All the chapters illustrate the way in which patients' mental states have an impact on their capacity to dream and to reflect on their dreams.

3) Dreams, transference, and counter-transference

In each of the chapters, the analysts' understanding of patients' dreams is crucially related to their sensitive attention to the experience of being with the patient in the consulting room. This, I think, is a radical contribution by analysts of the British Society, the way in which the free-floating attention of the analyst addresses—at times fragmented or undigested—experiences in the consulting room, or both the patient and analyst. One of the fun-damental assumptions, held by most analysts from all the groups in the British Society, is the understanding of the way a patient's internal world and his or her unconscious conflicts find expression in the relationship with the analyst, in the language of the transference. Understanding requires from the analyst the capacity to tolerate difficult and uncomfortable feelings, especially when patients project into the analyst aspects of themselves that are felt to be incompatible with the analyst's own views of themselves. The various chapters contain accounts of the ways in which the analysts processed these experiences and elaborated them within themselves, resisting the impulse to give them back immediately to their patients. This process of waiting is often a crucial pathway that leads to an understanding of the patient's anxieties. The analyst's task is to be receptive to those anxieties in the consulting room, to contain them and to be able to transform feelings and experiences into thoughts which are more bearable, so that the patient is able to think about them.

Sodré points out how her patient's unbearable experiences were dealt with by omnipotent obliteration. This was expressed powerfully in the transference, in the relationship with the analyst, who was left in doubt as to whether a specific experience in the transference had or had not taken place. It is the analyst's sensitive understanding of her experience in the counter-transference that informs her understanding of her patient and her dream. Sodré indicates that in her patient's analysis there is a shift towards a profound terror of depressive feelings and guilt.

Sedlak's chapter argues and illustrates the way that patients may project on to the analyst a dilemma which they are unable to dream about, so that the analyst's functioning may transform the dilemma into one that can be thought and dreamt about. He further argues that some patients have a developmental need to engage the analyst in this way.

In my chapter, I indicate how, in each of the three cases discussed, it was the experience I had of being with my patients (as well as my conceptual frames of reference) that ultimately allowed me to find meaning in their dreams. Maria's dream about a falling block of cement was integrated into my experience of feeling flattened in her presence, empty of thoughts, feelings, and associations. It was only then that an interpretation could be formulated and put to the patient.

Fonagy indicates how he needed briefly to become what Ms R wanted of him in order to be able to understand her.

In this book, dreams are understood as allowing access to a theory of mind, to the ways in which analysands conceive of their own mental lives, particularly their experiences of their inner world of thoughts and feelings. And understanding of the type of mental constructs presented by patients—i.e. the quality and content of their dreams, daydreams, thoughts or actions—at each moment in an analytic session is an important means of identifying the structure of their mental states. Dreams provide a language for the elaboration of conflicts, and contrast with daydreams that offer a phantasy of omnipotent wish fulfilment (Freud, 1900; Segal, 1980b; Winnicott, 1971). In the process, as Shoshana Felman (1993, pp. 122–123) has suggested, dreams "are susceptible of telling us about our own biography another story than the one we know or had believed to be our own".

The collection of contributions in this book indicates the multiplicity of pathways that allow the psychoanalyst to understand patients' dreams. The material from which understanding is derived is no longer contained in the patient's association only, but also lies in the experience of being with the patient in the consulting room, the state of mind that is evoked in the analyst himself, the atmosphere created, the subtle enactments that take place, and are progressively understood in the language of transference and counter-transference. In the process of their writing, the authors also raise issues of technique. Fonagy warns against over-interpreting; Flanders emphasizes that one is referring to psychoanalytic treatment, in that the continuity of daily sessions allows for a narrative to be constructed between the material of the preceding session and that of the following session. Sodré warns us that when guilt is experienced as too persecuting, "confronting one's patient prematurely with responsibility for the damage done to the object can lead to an increase of violence and the need to annihilate the object".

*   *   *

There are many other themes to which this book offers a contribution; not all of them can be tackled in this brief introduction. For example, the difference in manic defences against persecutory guilt in the paranoid schizoid and depressive positions (Sodré); dreams as expressing manic defences against unbearable guilt (Sodré and Flanders); the relevance of the repetition compulsion in the analysis of dreams (Perelberg), as well as issues of technique (Sodré, Sedlak, Kohon, Fonagy, Flanders, Perelberg). These and many other themes can be encountered in the reading of the rich contribution of each individual chapter.

A century later, a great deal has changed since Freud's *The Interpretation of Dreams*. What is the same, however, is the acknowledgement of the element of surprise, of the unexpected, which he so long ago defined as the hallmark of the unconscious, and which is still at the core of an analysis.

References

Bion, W. (1970). *Attention and Interpretation*. London: Karnac.

Britton, R. (1999). *Belief and Imagination* (New Library of Psycho-Analysis 31). London: Routledge.

Byatt, A. S., & Sodré, I. (1995). *Imagining Characters: Six Conversations about Women Writers*. London: Vintage.

Feldman, M. (1997). Projective identification: the analyst's involvement. *International Journal of Psycho-Analysis, 78*(2): 227–241.

Felman, S. (1993). *What Does a Woman Want?* Baltimore MD: Johns Hopkins University.

Flanders, S. (Ed.) (1993). *The Dream Discourse Today* (New Library of Psycho-Analysis 17). London: Routledge and The Institute of Psycho-Analysis.

Fonagy, P., & Target, M. (1995). Understanding the violent patient: the use of the body and the role of the father. *International Journal of Psycho-Analysis, 76*(3): 487–501 [also in Perelberg, R. J. (Ed.) (1999). *Psychoanalytic Understanding of Violence and Suicide* (New Library of Psycho-Analysis 33). London: Routledge and The Institute of Psycho-Analysis].

Freud, S. (1900). *The Interpretation of Dreams. S.E.*, 4 and 5.

Freud, S. (1914). *Remembering, Repeating and Working Through. S.E.*, 7.

Freud, S. (1917a). *The Unconscious. S.E.*, 14.

Freud, S. (1917b). *Mourning and Melancholia. S.E.*, 14.

Freud, S. (1920). *Beyond the Pleasure Principle. S.E.*, 18.

Freud, S. (1923). *Remarks on the Theory and Practice of Dream Interpretation. S.E.*, 19.

Freud, S. (1932). *New Introductory Lectures on Psychoanalysis. S.E.*, 22.

Green, A. (1986). *On Private Madness*. London: Hogarth and The Institute of Psycho-Analysis.

Green, A. (2000). *La Diachronie en Psychoanalyse*. Paris: Minuit.

Joseph, B. (1985). Transference: the total situation. In: E. Spillius, (Ed.), *Melanie Klein Today, Volume 2, Mainly Practice*. London: Routledge and the Institute of Psycho-Analysis.

Khan, M. M. R. (1962). Dream psychology and the evolution of the psychoanalytic situation. *International Journal of Psycho-Analysis*, 43 [reprinted in Flanders, S (Ed.) (1993). *op. cit.*].

Klein, M. (1927). Symposium on child analysis. In: *Writings, Volume 1* (pp. 139–169). London: Hogarth, 1975.

Lewin, B. (1946). Sleep, the mouth and the dream screen. *Psychoanalytic Quarterly*, 25: 169–199.

Lewin, B. (1955). Dream psychology and the analytic situation. *Psychoanalytic Quarterly*, 25: 169–199.

Mannoni, O. (1968). *Freud*. Paris: Seuil.

Sandler, J. (1976). Counter-transference and role responsiveness. *International Review of Psycho-Analysis*, 3: 43–47.

Segal, H. (1980a). Notes on symbol formation. In: *The Work of Hanna Segal*. London: Free Associations [reprinted, 1986].

Segal, H. (1980b). The function of dreams. In: *The Work of Hanna Segal, op. cit.*

Sharpe, E. F. (1937). *Dream Analysis*. London: Maresfield [7th impression, 1988].

Stewart, H. (1973). The experiencing of the dream and the transference. *International Journal of Psycho-Analysis*, 54 [reprinted in Flanders, S. (Ed.) (1993). *op. cit.*].

Tonnesman, M. (1992). Comments on "Negation". *British Psycho-Analytical Society Bulletin*, 28(2).

Winnicott, C., Shepherd, R., & Davis, M. (Eds.) (1989). *Psychoanalytic Explorations*. London: Karnac.

Winnicott, D. W. (1971). *Playing and Reality*. London: Penguin.

CHAPTER ONE

Non vixit: a ghost story

Ignês Sodré

F
reud discovered that we unconsciously invent ghosts because of our sense of guilt in relation to the dead; our ambivalence turns them into, "evil demons that have to be dreaded"; the proof of their existence is their persistence in living in our memory (Freud, 1915). Ghosts are omnipotent internal persecutors, who have the power, through being remembered, of "reappearing at any time in cunning and plotting ways" (Klein, 1935). In the paranoid schizoid position, dread of ghosts comes from the fear of retribution. But at the threshold of the depressive position, part of the persecution comes from their power to inflict the terrible pain of guilt.

The subject of this paper is a particular kind of manic defence against guilt. According to Klein, guilt is unbearable when reparation is felt to be impossible; and unbearable guilt is, by definition, not experienced as guilt but as a persecution. The more damaged the object is felt to be, the more impotent the ego faced with the task of reparation. The dead object, in phantasy murdered by one's death wishes, comes back to haunt the mind in a tormenting way, since it cannot be made to live again, and cannot entirely die, that is to say, disappear from the internal world. I will suggest that, faced with such persecution, the ego resorts to extremely drastic defences, which, in severely pathological states, can lead to effectively destroying part of the mind.

Freud's dream, "Non Vixit" is about revenants—ghosts—and the wish to destroy them. I will discuss it here, as an illustration of the use of manic defences against persecutory guilt; I will argue that the "story" in the dream, the wishful phantasy, could be used as a model for the understanding of severely pathological manic defences against depressive affects which are felt to be unbearable.

Persecutory guilt belongs to the threshold of the depressive position, to the critical moment in which the ego, through an awareness of its own destructive feelings and a growing sense of causality, begins to have to acknowledge that it has damaged its object. The object's capacity to survive, and its tolerance and forgiveness are essential for the ego to feel able to make reparation. If the object is felt to be either too damaged or too vengeful, reparation becomes impossible and guilt becomes too persecuting, forcing a regression to more primitive states of mind. The impossibility of making reparation provokes despair, and a consequent hatred of the damaged object that is felt, by its mere existence in the mind, to cause terrible suffering. The superego, felt to be on the side of the damaged object, constantly torments the ego, that feels both unloved and undeserving of love. Hatred of the object and of the superego leads to an increase of guilt and persecution, as the more attacked the object is, the more evil the ego feels itself to be, and the more hated by the superego, which has by now become, to use Freud's words, "a pure culture of the death instinct". The ego may not survive if it "doesn't fend off its tyrant in time by the change round into mania" (Freud, 1923).

The deeper understanding of persecutory guilt has led to modifications in Kleinian technique: if guilt is too persecuting, and the superego too sadistic, confronting one's patient prematurely, with responsibility for the damage done to the object, can lead to an increase of violence and the need to annihilate the object. In Joseph's words, "despair breeds violence, violence breeds despair"; she describes an internal situation in which the defences "while aiming at warding off immediate anxiety and guilt, in fact increase it and thus create further vicious circles of violence and despair" (Joseph, 1989).

The movement towards taking responsibility for one's internal world is parallel to the development of the superego, from internal objects felt either as good or bad to an observer (benevolent or malevolent) that gradually becomes integrated as an observing part of the ego. At the threshold of the depressive position there is a constant shifting backwards and forwards from, "It is my fault" to "it is not my fault". "It is not my fault" has two sources: the wish to be good and thus loved by the superego, and the wish to avoid the knowledge of having caused pain to the object. The inflexible avoidance of responsibility for what happens in internal reality leads to splitting the superego into an idealizing and a persecuting one (into lawyers for the defence and the prosecution, as it were), but also to a split in the ego in which the internal observer, the ego's capacity to know itself, is attacked. Violence is, therefore, directed not only against the persecuting object and the persecuting superego, but also against the functioning of the mind.

The patient I will discuss presents us with this problem: she is a very disturbed young woman, who deals with an underlying paranoid state by massive manic defences, whose inner world is dominated by violence and cruelty, and whose capacity for insight is practically non-existent. As the analysis proceeded, the sense of intense persecution defended against by such extreme manoeuvres seemed to shift from the fear and hatred of cruel internal objects, to what amounted, I think, to a terror of depressive feelings—ultimately a terror of guilt.

In Freud's ghost story, his dream, the real persecutor is the superego; "Non Vixit" is a confirmation, and I think a brilliant illustration, of his concept of mania: that the dramatic movement away from terrible persecution from a sadistic superego and into mania, i.e. a triumph over the superego, takes place via a fusion between the ego and the superego. I am going to show how this mechanism, which Freud uses in the dream, is used constantly, and pathologically, by my patient against her objects and, ultimately, against herself. My patient, I think, fights her ghosts by destroying the place where they live: her own mind.

Freud's "cocaine" dreams

The dream I want to examine, "Non Vixit", is essentially about persecutory guilt, and concerns Freud's sense of responsibility for hastening the death of his friend Fleischl by recommending cocaine as a cure for his morphine addiction. A lot has been written about this period in Freud's life (Bernfeld, 1953; Jones, 1953; Grinstein, 1930; Anzieu, 1986, etc.), so I will just summarize a few points that will be particularly helpful as a background for the dream.

The *dramatis personae* in the dream are Professor Fleischl and Joseph Paneth, both of whom, like Freud, had worked in Brucke's laboratory, and Fliess, Freud's closest friend. Ernst Fleischl was a brilliant man, who Freud admired and loved, and who became a helpful, generous friend. As is well known, in the course of his anatomical researches Fleischl developed a serious infection of a thumb which required an amputation and several operations, and left him permanently a victim of torturing pain; in trying to deal with this pain Fleischl eventually developed a severe morphine addiction.

When Freud first became interested in cocaine, two thoughts became the motivation for further pursuit in researching what he believed to be a "magical" drug: the thought of making a scientific breakthrough that would lead him to his becoming famous and therefore rich enough to be able to marry, and the thought of providing relief for his dear friend. In his letters to Martha, these thoughts often appear together. His admiration for Fleischl was such that he felt he had to reassure Martha that she needn't be jealous; and one of his letters contains a long, clearly oedipal, daydream, in which he considers Fleischl the ideal partner for Martha, and which ends in an oedipal triumph: "Why shouldn't I have more than I deserve?"

"Uber Coca", was published in July 1884; in September Freud left for a holiday with Martha, and when he came back, Koller, one of the people to whom he casually suggested the possible use of cocaine as an anaesthetic, had become internationally famous for, in fact, discovering the efficacy of cocaine as an anaesthetic in eye surgery. Freud later blamed Martha for his having missed the opportunity to become famous, suggesting that if he had not left Vienna to go on a holiday with her, he would have continued his research. I think the more likely unconscious motivation for blaming her is the fact that the urgency to publish "Uber Coca" was to do with the urgency of his wish to marry.

In *Uber Coca* Freud proclaims the virtues of cocaine against many things including depression; he writes about the "gorgeous excitement" it produces, even though he claims it produces a "normal" state of mind; and he tells Martha, "In my last depression I took coca again and a small dose lifted me to the heights in a wonderful fashion. I am just now busy collecting the literature for a song of praise for this magical substance" (E. Freud, 1960).

Fleischl, to whom Freud recommended cocaine as a cure for his morphine addiction, became a patient in "Uber Coca", providing the necessary evidence for the efficacy of the new drug. He held on to it "like a drowning man", was soon injecting massive doses of it, and became addicted. Freud was extremely distressed by his friend's state, and often refers to this in his letters to Martha. I think his guilt about professional misconduct, which appears so clearly in his "cocaine" dreams, with its underlying oedipal guilt, is accentuated by the link between being made famous by publishing Fleischl's "case" and the idea that this would make it possible to marry.

Freud's two "cocaine dreams": "Irma's injection" and "The botanical monograph", are dreams in which he is, essentially, dealing with guilt (Anzieu, 1986; Grinstein, 1980). In the dream "Irma's injection" Freud tries to prove that it is not his fault that his patient, instead of being cured, has become more ill. (This was later analyzed as his guilt, and Fliess's guilt, at the latter's careless nose operation on one of Freud's patients.) He associates the white patches in Irma's throat directly with cocaine and with the hastening of the death of "a dear friend" (Fleischl). In his associations, there is a very important slip (Jones, Bernfeld): "I had been the first to recommend the use of cocaine, in 1885, and this recommendation had brought serious reproaches down on me" (Freud, 1900). "Uber Coca" had been published in July 1884. The year 1885 is connected both to the recommendation of cocaine injections and to Fleischl's state: he had become possibly the first cocaine addict in Europe; in June 1885 he was desperately ill with cocaine intoxication, hallucinating, and suffering; Freud describes one of the many nights he spent with this dear friend as "the worst in his life". This dream ends, as you remember, with the thought, "Injections of that sort ought not to be made so thoughtlessly ... And probably the syringe had not been clean".

Anzieu's (1986) illuminating analysis of this dream shows it to be a trial, where "Freud stands accused by overwhelming evidence". "The question that lies at the heart of the tragedy, or the investigation, is now openly posed: who is responsible?" And he concludes (p. 140) "[...] the emphasis he puts on his own guilt feelings is important to him, for it constitutes his first self-analytic discovery about himself".

The dream of "The botanical monograph" is associated both with thoughts about the completion of *The Interpretation of Dreams* and to the coca monograph. About it Freud says, "once again the dream, like the one we first analyzed—the dream of Irma's injection—turns out to be in the nature of a self-justification [...]". Hamlet, interestingly enough, comes into his mind, as he quotes, in relation to the apparently innocent content of the dream: "There needs no ghost, my lord, come from the grave, to tell us this". The power of ghosts, in a dream that is to "help him overcome an inner conspiracy of doubts and reproaches" (Anzieu, *ibid.*, p. 289), is verified by a further association: "The thoughts corresponding to [the Botanical Monograph dream] consisted of a passionately agitated plea on behalf of my liberty to act as I chose to act and to govern my life as it seemed right to me and me alone. The dream that arose from them had an indifferent ring about it: 'I had written a monograph; it lay before me; it contained coloured plates; dried plants accompanied each copy'. This reminds one of the peace that has descended upon a battlefield strewn with corpses; no trace is left of the struggle which raged over it". No trace (...) except the corpses! I think this is a direct association to the "dried (i.e. dead) plants that accompanied each copy": the ghosts that appear again and again telling the same story.

"Non Vixit" belongs with these two "cocaine" dreams; but here the ghosts appear more explicitly in the manifest content of the dream, which was dreamt two or three days after a ceremony to unveil a memorial for Fleischl. This is its full text:

> I had gone to Brucke's laboratory at night, and, in response to a gentle knock on the door, I opened it to (the late) Professor Fleischl, who came in with a number of strangers, and, after exchanging a few words, sat down at his table.

This was followed by a second dream.

> My friend Fl. [Fliess] had come to Vienna unobtrusively in July. I met him in the street in conversation with my (deceased) friend P.

[Paneth], and went with them to some place where they sat opposite each other as though they were at a small table. I sat in front at its narrow end. Fl. [Fliess] spoke about his sister and said that in three-quarters of an hour she was dead, and added some such words as "that was the threshold". As P. [Paneth] failed to understand him, Fl. [Fliess] turned to me and asked him how much I had told P. [Paneth] about his affairs. Whereupon, overcome by strange emotions, I tried to explain to Fl. [Fliess] that P. [Paneth] (could not understand anything at all, of course, because he) was not alive. But what I actually said—and I myself noticed the mistake—was, "NON VIXIT". ["He has not lived"]. I then gave P. [Paneth] a piercing look. Under my gaze he turned pale; his form grew indistinct and his eyes a sickly blue—and finally he melted away. I was highly delighted at this and I now realized that Ernst Fleischl, too, had been no more than an apparition, a "revenant"; and it seemed to me quite possible that people of that kind only existed as long as one liked and could be got rid of if someone else wished it.

Freud continues:

This fine specimen includes many of the characteristics of dreams— the fact that I exercised my critical faculties during the dream and myself noticed my mistake when I said "Non vixit" instead of "Non vivit", my unconcerned dealings with people who were dead and were recognized as being dead in the dream itself, the absurdity of my final inference and the great satisfaction it gave me. This dream exhibits so many of these puzzling features, indeed, that I would give a great deal to be able to present the complete solution of its conundrums. *I am incapable of doing so—of doing, that is to say, what I did in the dream, of sacrificing to my ambition people whom I greatly value.* Any concealment, however, would destroy what I know very well to be the dream's meaning; etc. [p. 549; my italics]

Freud associates the annihilation of Paneth with a look, to a scene in which Brucke, having found him (Freud) at fault, looked at him accusingly with his beautiful but terrible blue eyes, "by which I was reduced to nothing". He notes the similarity between Fleischl's name and Fliess, who was ill at the time, and who he had been consciously feeling guilty about. He associates "July" to Julius Caesar, and his playing the part of Brutus to his cousin John's Caesar: "And as he was ambitious, I slew him"—and links this to Paneth's death wishes in relation to Fleischl (so he could take his place at Brucke's laboratory). In short, he analyses this as the projection of his murderous wishes into P., who had also died, and whom he had also been thinking about during the memorial ceremony for Fleischl. The accusation of indiscretion is associated to a current situation related to Fliess and a past situation, involving Fleischl and Breuer when he was, in fact, indiscreet. Later he comments on his feeling "highly delighted" "to approve the possibility, which in waking life I knew was absurd, of there being revenants who could be eliminated by a mere wish": "*This satisfaction, of being left in possession of the field, constituted the major part of the affect of the dream*".

As we have seen, in the text of *The Interpretation of Dreams*, the first comment Freud makes is, that he is incapable of doing what he did in the dream: "of sacrificing to my ambition people whom I greatly value". I agree with Grinstein (1980) who suggests this should be thought of as an association. And what I find striking is that Freud absolutely takes it for granted, before any explanation, that we can see this is what he did in the dream, when this is not part of the conscious dream text. In the dream the attack follows an accusation of indiscretion, not ambition. Freud's immediate claim of innocence—"I am incapable of doing [such a thing]!"—amounts to an unconscious confession. In relation to Fleischl and the cocaine situation, though, indiscretion and ambition come together: to prove the efficacy of cocaine against morphine addiction, Freud describes a patient, who, in reality, was Fleischl.

I think it is clear that omnipotence is resorted to when guilt of a persecutory nature is overwhelming. Anzieu (1986), in a footnote to his analysis of "My uncle with the yellow beard" comments: "Freud eventually recognized his own megalomaniac wish, but did not, I would contend, succeed in seeing it as a megalomaniac defence against persecutory anxiety". In this context, though, he is, I suspect, aware that the megalomania is a defence against the persecution of the accusing blue eyes. In this dream, it is clear that he does not just project the guilt (as he does in "Irma's injection"); he can only deal with the accusation by becoming omnipotent.

Grinstein interprets "July" in relation to Freud's younger brother Julius, who died in infancy, and who was born in the same year as Paneth, the other revenant. He thinks that the mention of Fliess's sister, who also died in infancy, confirms this. The link is thus made with Freud's first "ghost", whose death must have confirmed for the boy, Freud, the omnipotence of his death wishes. It is quite clear, in the focus of his interpretations, that Freud wants us to see the dream as one that is centrally about rivalry, and that he disguises (only just) what the real guilt is about.

I think, "Fl. came to Vienna unobtrusively in July", is also connected to the date of publication of the Coca monograph—a date important in itself—and also the point of the curious parapraxis I already mentioned. The cocaine paper came to Vienna much too "unobtrusively", compared to Koller's, when he missed his chance of fame. And much too obtrusively when it became infamous, as he was accused of causing the advent of "the third scourge of humanity", and, especially, in his own eyes for contributing to the Fleischl tragedy.

I think, in this context, what Freud considers the main affect of the dream—the satisfaction of "being left in possession of the field"—goes beyond the triumph over rivals that Freud is directly addressing. I think it indicates the wish *to be left in full possession of his mind*—the ego must triumph over the dead objects that have invaded the mind, by making them disappear, not just now and forever, but also to make them not to have ever existed, so they cannot return to haunt him. And ultimately, the ego must triumph over the tormenting superego, that is felt here as a life threatening enemy: "he reduced me to nothing", as he would later brilliantly expose in his papers on depression and the superego. The ego triumphs via a massive projective identification with the aggressor: the omnipotently sadistic superego. Omnipotence is required to undo the past in a concrete way. "If he has never existed, then, of course, I cannot have killed him!" is Freud's wishful phantasy in his dream.

Clinical material

Miss A is the eldest of three children; both her parents seem quite disturbed. The father is Jewish and the sole survivor of the holocaust in his immediate family: his mother, father and sister died in a concentration camp. Before the war, he had been sent to another country where he was brought up. He never referred to the past, so his children, until they grew up, did not even know that he was Jewish. He seems to be a grandiose, manic man, who apparently had a very excited relationship with his daughter when she was very small, but had then withdrawn his interest. He was promiscuous, left his wife more than once when the children were small, and finally left when my patient was a teenager. The mother was often depressed and sometimes violent. She apparently used to forget her daughter in the garden when she was a young infant, and once nearly caused the baby to freeze to death. She told her daughter that she was a strange child, who even as an infant hated to be touched or picked up. Just before ending her analysis, my patient told me, in a casual way, that her mother had had a psychotic breakdown after her birth, in which she had the delusional belief that she had been pregnant with twins, and that the doctors had killed the other baby, a boy.

Miss A had known this for many years, but it had never occurred to her to tell me. Much has been written about the children of holocaust survivors (Pines, 1993), and the kind of projections to which they are constantly exposed; the mother's breakdown seemed to add to and confirm this experience, my patient being the survivor of a "concentration camp" in her mother's mind.

Miss A suffered from an almost total childhood amnesia; her handful of "memories", offered to me as a handful of rather meaningless photographs in the beginning of the analysis, did not seem to become integrated into her experience of herself. In the analysis she very rarely referred to the past. She also had what she called "a very bad memory" for present day events; she often forgot not only the entire content of her sessions, but even whether she had had a session in the previous day or not (she often missed). But above all she suffered from an emotional amnesia: if I reminded her of rather critical events, for instance, that the boyfriend who seems so sweet had very recently beaten her up and nearly murdered her, she would "remember" as if this event was a film on television: the "tape" hadn't been entirely erased, but the feelings had, so totally that she could not make contact with them.

Something she did remember, however, was a thought she had had soon after her brother was born, when she was four-years-old: the parents had left her "looking after him" in the bedroom when they were somewhere else, and she thought, "They must be mad! I could so easily kill him!" The feeling was of triumph and contempt for her stupid parents.

In the sessions she seemed most of the time to be "mindless", talking about hollow, empty, repetitive things, in a more or less chronically hypomanic way, showing no interest at all in what I had to say, or in her own states of mind. She felt she had absolutely no relationship with me, and my sense of a lack of reality in the transference was such, that sometimes I doubted its existence; at the time, I described this as an "invisible transference". These "empty" states changed to states of violent rage and pain in relation to her boyfriends who always turned out to be psychopaths, unfaithful to her, and unreliable in every way. She moved from having fantasies of killing her father to wanting to kill her boyfriend, who became more and more violent and criminal. But this criminality was tremendously exciting and she became gradually more and more involved in life in the underworld, as it were. Except for momentary crises of rage and terrible distress at being cheated, life in the underworld was felt as quite wonderful.

As a defence against terror, but also against the intense persecution caused by the emergence of depressive affects (sorrow, grief, and guilt) my patient discovered, or created, a world of criminals, in which she felt quite at ease by a manic projective identification with the omnipotent "baddies". Being friendly with petty criminals, who were sometimes violent, she also got to know more dangerous criminals, who were the "stars" in this environment. In other words: she created, in external reality, a place to project the concentration camp, or the inside of the mother where murders take place, and in this world she lived most of the time in a manic state, identified with the murderers. The past did not exist, and yet at the same time had to be repeated concretely in the present, through her living in this criminal world which was constantly erotized, and felt to be under her omnipotent control.

My patient seemed to have no sense of an integrated past, nor a sense of a continuum from her child self to her adult self; her past was not a memory, but a horrible nightmare that was dealt with by recreating it in an external reality over which, in phantasy, she had more control. As the analysis proceeded, she dealt with the rudiments of depressive affect (loss, even guilt of a very primitive kind) by making her internal experiences meaningless. But there were moments in which something moving happened that convinced me that there was more contact with herself and with me. Then this experience seemed suddenly to disappear and I would become convinced that *what I thought had happened had in fact never happened: Non Vixit!*

For example: she started a session in what seemed to be an unusual mood; she was quiet, seemed sad, and eventually told me that she had been feeling very lonely, even though D, her boyfriend, had been there. She had not been able to sleep at all; she was so tired, "today is going to be a nightmare!" A small object had got broken, and D had promised to buy glue to fix it. But he is so false! He had had a tube of glue in his pocket all week; she had discovered it when looking in his pocket for clues of his infidelity [he is often unfaithful, which causes her to become violent and very distressed]. She now began to talk about him in an angry but also very excited way; I thought she was whipping up some powerful excitement against the unusual sense of loneliness and of sadness about something broken. [Often with this patient what appears as a triangular situation of intense jealousy, which tends to be immediately erotized so that I seem to be witnessing a sadomasochistic orgy, is a defence against a situation of extreme loneliness in the presence of an object whose mind is entirely occupied with something else—not necessarily a rival, and not necessarily exciting or good. "Jealousy" and "infidelity" also serve to "name" a more primitive and incomprehensible experience.] She said that there is nothing she likes about D, she wishes she could break up with him. He is so false and tricky, and lies all the time. After a pause, she said somebody had lent her a book about a woman who took Valium for ten years—when she stopped she went mad. I said there is a horrible relationship to which she feels addicted, and she fears something much worse (mad) if she leaves it. I thought that she felt that I did not realize how dangerous it would be for her to leave that to which she is addicted. She then said that D had insisted on having the phone number of my consulting room, so he can 'phone her here, and she had given it to him. She thinks this was a mad thing to have done.

Reading the book about the woman addicted to a drug, which also describes this woman's experiences with psychotherapy, made her think that perhaps if she thought more about her past it could help her analysis. [This again was rather unusual, as she had never shown any intellectual curiosity about analysis, and had never referred to helping the process in any way.]

After a pause, she said rather flippantly: "I usually don't think about the past, I just dismiss it!", and I said I thought her past was not easily available to her, but that she prefers to think that she just dismisses it. The forgotten past, in the session, seems to be a feeling of loneliness and sadness at something broken; what seems to be available and invited into the session, like D, is something disruptive and false, but exciting, that pushes everything else out. And yet I thought that she felt pained at being disconnected from herself. She said, "I have five or ten memories, that's all". She paused, then added, "But I just remembered something now! Did I ever tell you about my favourite toy when I was little, a Mickey Mouse doll? I really loved it. But one day my mother washed it and it disintegrated completely. I remember so clearly now, being in the cot, looking through the bars, crying for my doll. Did I ever tell you about Hank? (She hadn't.) It was a beautiful cowboy doll, with arched legs for riding—very well designed, beautiful colours. But my mother tried to trick me with it—pretending Mickey had never existed, for me to have Hank instead. It was a hollow rubber doll, like those toys for dogs to chew on. My mother used to say really strange things to me". She pauses, then says, in a pained voice, "Why don't I ever remember my childhood?"

There was something very moving in all this; I felt sad for this little girl in the cot, and also hopeful: it seemed possible to make contact with the state of mind in the beginning of the session. I proceeded to interpret along the lines of her story: her sense of loss of the past but also of herself, the constant "drugging" of herself by becoming attached to the exciting, but hollow, "doll". [I was thinking of the constant whipping up of manic and intensely erotized relationships with bad objects.] When I mentioned something important and loved, which she feels exists only for a moment and then gets disintegrated, she interrupted, in an excited voice: "Do you know something? The expression 'Mickey Mouse' in the East End means false, a fake! [she laughs] For instance, a mickey mouse gold watch would be a fake gold one!" I felt shocked—as if I had been in a different world, probably of my own invention, and had been brought back to the brutal reality.

Later on, when writing about this session, I felt that my own need to hold on to something more hopeful had caused me to idealize something called a childhood memory, as if it was gold. I felt I had been out of touch with my patient; but also angry, as if I had been offered a toy, only to have it disintegrate in front of my eyes. After all, I had been told that a false, tricky character had been (literally) invited into the session. What a fool I was! And yet, as I had to remind myself, my patient had also told me: "On the other hand, this isn't a good example, because mickey mouse watches really exist—those watches for children, with the Mickey mouse picture in them—and therefore, those aren't fake".

This material can, of course, be examined and interpreted in many different ways. However, I want to focus on the disintegration of anything that leads to the experiencing of the depressive affect. In her manic mood, the patient is projectively identified with an internal object who attacks and disintegrates any connection with something meaningful; my experience in the session seems to be that what I thought was happening had not happened: it has never happened at all. This kind of denial of loss (you cannot lose what has never existed), obliterates the lost object through total annihilation. What seems different in the use of such massive manic defences is that the depressive affect is not just avoided, made unimportant, triumphed over etc.—but my experience, in the session, is much more like "non vixit": it has never happened. The patient in the session seems to be projectively identified with a parent who "non vixits" the past. The disintegrated object presumably returns to haunt her as ghostly fragments that have to be dealt with again and again by annihilation; mindlessness is the only safe state in which to be.

The tragedy of this situation is, I think, very clearly illustrated in a dream from around the same time:

Towards the end of the session that preceded this dream, she told me, in her usual casual way, that she had met, for the first time, some relatives of her Father's: an uncle and an aunt who had lived in another country since before the War, and who had managed to trace her family in this country, and had come to London specially to meet them [she had never mentioned them before now]. They were surprised that her father had never tried to get in touch with them. She had gone out with her brother and her sister to have a meal with this couple, who had shown a lot of interest in them. She had thought, "Maybe I could get to love this uncle!", but quickly dismissed the thought as very silly, since he would probably die soon, anyway. She found herself looking, in a fascinated way, at his hands when he was eating: how difficult it was for him to cut his food, his hands seemed so fragile, so thin and old and wrinkled. Her detailed description was almost overwhelmingly painful to me. She then said he had showed her a photograph of her grandmother, who had died in the concentration camp. She was quiet for a minute or two, and then said: "When he showed it to me, I thought I was going to cry! Can you imagine it? How incredibly false! How sentimental! I don't care much even for my other grandmother, who is alive! Why should I care for this one, who is dead?" She proceeded to tell me that the meal was great, that she had chosen her favourite food, which was, of course, the most expensive thing on the menu, lobster, and that she had totally enjoyed it. It was the end of the session, and she left with a big smile.

She started the next session by telling me a dream (an extremely rare event).

In the dream, she was in an aeroplane, feeling perfectly relaxed, not at all afraid. [She has been very afraid of flying, but here she interrupts to tell me that when she flew last summer, for the first time she hadn't been at all afraid.] Next to her plane there was another plane, which was clearly in great danger; but somehow in the dream this did not seem to matter at all to her. The other plane was upside down, and turning round and round very fast. The passengers seemed unaware of what was going on; only the pilot knew what was happening, he knew they were going to crash, but he was totally powerless to prevent it. Looking through the windows she could see among the passengers an old lady and a little child; she was like a grandmother, looking after the child; she got up, perhaps to take the child to the toilet. When she woke up she knew that in seconds the plane would have completely disintegrated.

I think that at the point in the analysis when a connection began to be forged (however tenuous and short-lived) between the sense of loss and the horrible damage done to her internal objects, the depressive affect became intensely persecuting. The projective identification with the aggressor, the parent who destroys links in internal reality, and who presumably projects ghostly experiences, has now the function not only to protect her from terror, but also of doing away with her destroyed, suffering internal objects that haunt her with pain and despair. A vicious cycle of violence ensues, in which the more damaged the object, the more it needs to be killed. I attempted to show that the way of dealing with this in the sessions was by unconsciously communicating to me a depressive experience so that it could be "non-vixied" in my mind. I emphasize that a communication of the depressive affects takes place, because something remains in my mind even if it has been obliterated from hers. For instance, I know that a little child and a grandmother once got together even if, like the pilot, I am powerless to prevent my patient from removing herself to another plane where death is exciting, nothing matters, and the part of her mind that feels pain is disintegrated. When my patient turns into a lobster, at tremendous cost to her personality, she does not only protect herself with a thick carapace; she also murders her objects and the part of herself that is attached to them. As in Joseph's formulation, sadism has to be ever increasing to avoid guilt and despair.

To sum up: in a normal mourning process, in the depressive position, guilt for the damage inflicted on the object, now lost, has to be faced, to permit a process of internalization to take place in which the object gradually becomes established in the internal world. Loss and responsibility for ambivalence have to be accepted so that the object can live in memory. But when guilt is unbearable, and the damage inflicted on the object is felt to be irreparable, manic defences are used pathologically, to annihilate the object. The inner world becomes populated with ghosts, rather than with memories, and the capacity to perceive internal reality has to be constantly attacked. At the threshold of the depressive position, the paranoid fear of retribution—"an eye for an eye"—becomes the fear of the superego's accusing eyes, as well as the hatred for the mind's eye, which is tormented by the ghostly sight of suffering internal objects.

References

Anzieu, D. (1986). *Freud's Self-Analysis*. London: The Hogarth Press and the Institute of Psycho-Analysis.

Bernfeld, S. (1953). Freud's studies on cocaine, 1884–1887. *Journal of the American Psychoanalytic Association*, I(4).

Freud, E. (1960). *The Letters of Sigmund Freud*. New York: Basic Books.

Freud, S. (1884). Uber coca. In: R. Byck (Ed.), *The Cocaine Papers*. Vienna: Dunquin, 1963.

Freud, S. (1900). *The Interpretation of Dreams*. S.E., 4 and 5.

Freud, S. (1915). *Thoughts For the Times of War and Death*. S.E., 14.

Freud, S. (1923). *The Ego and the Id*. S.E., 19.

Grinstein, A. (1980). *Sigmund Freud's Dreams*. New York: International Universities Press.

Jones, E. (1953). *Sigmund Freud: Life and Work*. London: Hogarth Press.

Joseph, B. (1989). Despair breeds violence; violence breeds despair, unpublished.

Klein, M. (1935). A contribution to the psychogenesis of manic-depressive states. In: *The Writings of Melanie Klein, Volume 1*. London: The Hogarth Press and The Institute of Psycho-Analysis.

Pines, D. (1993). The impact of the holocaust in the second generation. In: *A Woman's Unconscious Use of her Body*. London: Virago Press.

CHAPTER TWO

The dream space and counter-transference

Victor Sedlak

Introduction

L ewin's (1946, 1953) introduction of the concept of the dream
screen was an attempt to investigate the nature of the space
in which the dream is created and experienced. He
appeared to conceptualize a two-dimensional entity, having its
genesis in the infant's perception of the surface of the maternal
breast, onto which dream images could be projected. Although
Lewin's contribution was important in opening up an area of
research, it is probably true to say that its clinical significance was
limited. Further developments have tended to describe a three-
dimensional space with capacities, for example, for toleration of the
frustration of foregoing the concrete satisfaction of reality, and for
symbolic elaboration (Khan, 1962, 1972). The images used to convey
this internal space are, in contrast to that of a screen, more
suggestive of a three-dimensional entity, for example, a psychic
envelope (Anzieu, 1989). As Khan (1972) noted: "The dream screen
is something onto which the dream imagery is projected, whereas
the dream space is a psychic area in which the dream process is
actualised into experiential reality".

Another of Lewin's seminal contributions has led to the comparison being made between a patient's experience of a dream and the experience of an analytic session. He argued (Lewin, 1955) that the analytic situation arose when the patient's resistance was too great to allow himself to be put into the sleep-like state of hypnosis. It was Freud's genius to have created a situation in which some of the aspects of sleep were recreated (e.g. the freedom to allow one's mind to wander with some diminution of repressive forces), while other inhibitions against such regression were respected. There is now a considerable literature comparing the situation of the dreamer with that of the analysand, which demonstrates the similarities of the ego capacities involved in the creative use of dreaming and of an analytic session. Correspondingly, the similar emotional and cognitive difficulties that result in an incapacity to use these situations creatively have also been noted. A number of analysts (Gammill, 1980; Khan, 1972; Stewart, 1973) have reported a significant improvement in a patient's capacity to dream creatively following analytic work, which has led to a beneficial change in the transference relationship. In this paper, I am distinguishing between a creative use of a dream and the other uses that a dream can be put to (Khan, 1972; Segal, 1981). My interest is in the former use.

I intend to link the patient's capacity to create a dream with the state of the analyst's counter-transference. It is interesting to note that a change in the conceptualization of the analyst's task has paralleled that of the dream space. This began with the expanded understanding of the counter-transference response as a possible means of comprehending the patient's material (Heiman, 1950). This, together with the increasing use of the concept of projective identification, has led to a view of the analyst's functioning in terms of a three-dimensional containment of projections and away from the provision of oneself as a blank screen onto which the patient projects. A number of analysts (e.g. Brenman Pick, 1985; Carpy, 1989; Joseph, 1989; Sandler, 1976) have described the ways in which a patient subtly demands and emotionally presses the analyst to enact various behaviours, often employing conscious and unconscious perceptions of the analyst's personality in order to effect this. However, if the analyst is able to differentiate between his personal qualities and the way that they are being used by the patient to coerce the analyst into some enactment, understand why this is happening, and put this into words, then considerable analytic development can ensue. This is indeed difficult, not least because the counter-transference is primarily an unconscious response.

In my mind, the topic of counter-transference is also associated with some observations made to me by a senior colleague (O'Shaughnessy, 1993, personal communication). Having been impressed with how perspicaciously she had understood some material in supervision (material which had left me in a state of confusion), I wondered, out loud, how my patient might have fared if my supervisor had been his analyst. This led us on to discuss the advantages that the supervisor has in terms of, for example, greater clinical experience. She also noted that often the supervisee has consciously or unconsciously done some processing of their counter-transference, so that some of the work in understanding has already been accomplished prior to the supervision, thus giving the supervisor greater access to the dynamics of the clinical situation. She added, however, that in her experience some patients soon come to know, unconsciously, the level of their analyst's understanding and then proceed to pitch their material beyond that point. In such a case, a supervisor's greater clinical experience may not have been of immediate help in the hypothetical situation of their having the patient in treatment.

In this paper, I wish to show via two detailed clinical examples how, in some cases at least, there is a fundamental relationship between the patient's capacity or incapacity to create a dream about a current emotional issue and the analyst's ability to work through that issue in the counter-transference. Furthermore, I will show that the patient may unconsciously produce in the analyst the very difficulty that they cannot dream about. My examples demonstrate how this is done in a very particular way, precisely enacted at the point at which the analyst's capacity to understand is, maybe for a considerable time, stretched beyond the level of comprehension. I will further argue that there is a developmental and analytic need for this to occur in certain circumstances.

First clinical illustration

This material is taken from the analysis of a professional man who was in his late thirties when he came into treatment.

He sought analysis to help him with a long standing depression which he dated back to his childhood. From what I could gather his parents had been disturbed in their own right. His mother appeared to take a paranoid view of the world, best exemplified by an early memory of him throwing a ball at a door and she accusing him of intending to hit her. She had suffered two major depressive breakdowns which had required hospitalization. The first of these was at the time of a move of house which closely followed the birth of his sister. He was then four. His father was described as a cold and controlling man. An older brother has been diagnosed as psychotic. His bleak emotionally cold childhood is best conveyed by his recollection of family meals which were silent sombre affairs at which his father, if in a bad mood, might snap at any member of the family who was eating "wrongly", although it was not clear to the patient quite what this eating wrongly entailed.

The session I am going to present occurred six months after the beginning of his analysis. These months had been notable for the extreme care he took in speaking to me, his slow ponderous accounts of what he had done the previous day and his inability to feel at ease or to say anything to me spontaneously. In this period he had only reported one dream in which he was standing in front of a mock Tudor house. His one association to this had been that he had always lived in Victorian houses and I had interpreted how he felt that he was, in the analysis, always confronted with a Victor who he felt was likely to mock him unless he was very careful about what he said. This interpretation had not relieved him, but had seemed to increase the care he took in speaking to me. In the transference, despite my sympathy for his plight, I would find myself bored, impatient, and frequently my concentration would wander. This session came just after a weekend and in the week before a three-week Easter break.

I had noticed his difficulty in speaking getting progressively worse as the break had approached and in the session prior to the weekend he had begun to say that at work he had felt angry but he had strangulated the work and said "ang ...". I was reminded of this, in this session, by his torturous way of speaking as he slowly described that over the weekend he had found himself very busy, doing too much, rushing around until he had a headache. I made a comment based on some material from the previous week about his anxiety of having too much time and feeling alone in an empty space. He responded to this by saying he was resigned to the Easter break, as one would be in a condemned cell. This remark led me to say that he felt Easter was the punishment for some crime he had committed. At this moment the patient spontaneously remembered a dream he had had the previous night.

He was walking along a railway line which ran along a raised embankment. Looking down he could see a robbery taking place, one man was stealing from another. Somehow his presence became known to the robber, he slipped down the embankment and found himself confronted by the robber, pointing a gun at him, about to shoot him. At this point the patient had woken feeling very anxious.

There was one association to the dream which was that as an adolescent the patient had been a keen train spotter. He and a friend had once walked across several lines which had been electrified, they had had to take great care in stepping over them and his friend had nearly tripped onto a live rail. This association seemed to contain such an accurate description of the great care the patient took in speaking to me that I interpreted that he felt he had to be extremely careful in what he told me of his thoughts, particularly in ensuring that he did not touch anything alive. I went on to suggest that the live emotion was the anger he felt about his belief that I was robbing him by taking a break, but that he was terrified to show this because he felt it would lead to a deadly confrontation.

The patient did not respond to this for a number of minutes, but he did shift around on the couch as if he was he was extremely uncomfortable. He then said "I feel hunted". The silence continued until, in a most hesitant way, he said that in the previous break he had felt nothing for a few days, but had then felt extremely irritated. This last word was said only after a struggle in which he stuttered and finally forced the word out. This noticeably increased his physical discomfort. I then interpreted that he felt that the dream had happened in the session: he had been progressing carefully, keeping his feelings about my robbing him to himself, but then he had slipped; he had remembered his dream and this had led me to see what his view of the situation was. He now felt that I had him in my sights and there was no escape. The patient's anxiety was not relieved by this interpretation, he repeated that he felt hunted and

chaotic and there the session finished. At the door the patient turned
to me in his habitual way to say "Goodbye" but this time said
"O.K., goodbye".

I have reported this material because I think it illustrates the way
that this patient was unable, at this time, to form a dream that
would depict his dilemma and would also serve the function of
preserving his sleep. His capacities to do this had broken down in
the night, his dream had changed into a nightmare which had
woken him. In precisely the same way, he was unable to maintain a
symbolic level of interchange with me in the session and he had
suddenly found himself in the middle of a situation in which he felt
concretely threatened. Although his saying "O.K." before "Goodbye" probably indicated that there still existed a part of his mind
that could maintain the idea that what had occurred had been
valuable, I think that, for the most part, he had felt concretely
involved in a dangerous confrontation.

It was only after some further months that I was able to see for
myself that my patient was actually putting me into the same
position as he had occupied in the dream and that, for a
considerable period of time, I was little better equipped to work
through this dilemma than he was himself. I slowly came to realize
that a regular counter-transferential experience was that I would
feel robbed of what I felt was rightfully mine, i.e. the patient's free
associations. This would often occur right at the beginning of a
session, when he would be silent but I would sense that he was
thoughtful. However, after a few minutes when he would begin to
speak it would be to say, in a most flat way, "Yesterday ..." and he
would then proceed to tell me what had happened the previous
day. This would soon leave me feeling bored and inattentive.
However, I would then be in a dilemma: if I tried to ignore this
feeling and make myself concentrate, I would find myself making
interpretations that felt sterile and lifeless (not surprisingly, since I
had taken care to avoid the live rail/dynamic). If I did try to take up
with him how he excluded me from his thinking, we would quickly
get into what felt like a more deadly confrontation in which he felt
very accused and caught out and would then proceed to berate
himself in a vicious way.

As I was trying to think my way through this dilemma, I had a dream about the patient. I dreamt that I was opening the door to him and, as I did so, he rushed past me and ran into the main part of the house. I was taken by surprise, felt shocked by the intrusion and quite unable to stop him. It was clear in the dream that, having rushed past me, the patient continued past the consulting room door and the waiting room entrance (in fact the first two doors in the hallway) and hence past the boundary in the hall between the space set aside for patients and the family living space.

As I thought about this dream, I came to realize that it depicted, very accurately, my difficulties with this patient. His intrusive projection regularly got beyond the point in my mind at which I could function as an analyst, i.e. use a mental consulting room in which to think about my experience or at least a waiting room in which I could sit comfortably with my thoughts until they became clearer. Once he had got past this point in my mind and into my personal space, in which I tend to turn a blind eye to provocation up to a point and beyond this to react aggressively, it was almost inevitable that I would enact my difficulty. I took great care not to do this, but would then find that this was not just a proper attempt to maintain a professional stance, but, in itself, a manifestation of the patient's projection (which had found its place in my personality) of a kind of emotional temerity. Thus, there were times when my interpretations either avoided the alive rail or touched it dangerously. In the latter times my interpretations could have an attacking and sometimes snide quality.

Over time, as I continued to think through my counter-transferential feelings, I was able to find ways of talking to him about the position he put me in and the way that it paralleled his own. I would interpret that, by these means, he was communicating to me both his sense of being robbed and his difficulty in experiencing it, in a way he could think about, that would enable him to communicate it by putting it into words. This period of work undoubtedly helped the patient become more communicative and spontaneous and I noted a greater ability to bring his dreams to the analysis.

It has not been my intention to present an overall view of an analysis, but rather to describe material that relates to the thesis of this paper. However, it may be of interest to know that the analysis ended prematurely, after three years, because of my decision to move away from London. The progress that had been made in that time enabled him to speak much more freely about his feelings including, of course, his sense that he was being robbed by the termination of his analysis. Poignantly he was able to link this to a childhood sense that he had been robbed of the experience of having a normal upbringing with normal parents.

Second clinical illustration

My second example of the link between a patient's inability to create a dream and the analyst's need to work through a difficulty that the patient creates in the counter-transference also comes from my own practice.

> Mr B came for analysis in his mid-forties. As a teenager and in his twenties, he had enjoyed phenomenal success as an entrepreneur and had in fact retired at the age of twenty eight. However, it was also at this time that his father had died and hence his retirement was open to the interpretation that he had suffered a breakdown at that point. This was very relevant to the time of his presenting himself for analysis, because his mother was then in her seventies and had been diagnosed as having an inoperable carcinoma. He told me in the consultation interview that he feared that he would not be able to cope with her death. He had also just suffered the breakdown of a relationship with a much younger, very glamorous woman who had left him for a younger man, a blow which had hit him very hard and which had also reinforced his anxieties about his aging. He claimed that it had also left him physically disfigured by two marks on his face. He complained, in his consultation, that his mother was unsympathetic to the pain this caused him and mocked him for wearing make-up to try and hide these marks.
>
> I do not intend to give a full account of the analysis up to the point at which the series of incidents I want to describe occurred. Suffice it to say that, in the first three years of the analysis, a convincing picture emerged of a man who was persecuted by an underlying phantasy that his resources could at any point be lost to him. In his childhood he had developed the habit of holding on to his stools and in adulthood he still took an exceptional interest in his toileting. He

worried obsessively about money, although he continued to be very comfortably off; he was extremely careful about expending his physical, mental, and emotional energies. He had very many complicated routines and rituals which were designed to save time, but which inevitably made him late for most appointments including his sessions. It could be said that Mr B was persecuted by time slipping away from him. Although he himself acknowledged that he had in effect spent sixteen years doing almost nothing, he told me that in that time he was forever racing against the clock and he once added, "I hardly had the time to wipe my arse".

As might be imagined Mr B hated paying for his analysis, particularly· for those rare sessions that he was unable to keep. Nevertheless, he did appear to make some progress in his life during the first three years of the treatment. His skin complaint quickly cleared up, he developed a new relationship with a woman only a little younger than himself, which was difficult and contained much acting out from the analysis, but as far as I could tell also had many good qualities. He also began, for the first time in about twenty years, to work again, on a much smaller scale than before but in a way that gave him much satisfaction, particularly when he could report that his earnings from this work more than covered the cost of the analysis.

During the first three years of the analysis his mother's health had slowly deteriorated. His attempts to take her to faith healers and to persuade her to try ever more far fetched therapies had slowly subsided in the face of analytic work and the reality of her deterioration. He slowly came to accept the fact of her approaching death and began to devote his energies, together with his two sisters, to making her last days as comfortable and as pain-free as they could arrange. One Friday morning a message was left on my answering machine by Mr B's partner to say that his mother was in the process of dying and he would not attend for his session.

He rang me that same afternoon to say that she had died in the morning at the time that his session began. We spoke for a few minutes and, in the course of our conversation, I said that the care that he and his sisters had given his mother in her last months (which had really impressed me very much) must have helped her enormously. He thanked me for this and for the help I had given him in facing his mother's death.

The following Monday Mr B told me that he had spoken to his partner about our telephone conversation and of his appreciation of what I had said to him. She had responded by saying "Oh yes, but he'll still charge you for the missed session". Mr B added that he had told her he knew that of course I would not do such a thing. Upon hearing this I immediately felt ambushed; I had always charged Mr B for missed sessions, it had always been a contentious issue and now I felt that he was taking advantage of these exceptional circumstances in order to make his long-held point that it was unfair of me to charge him for missed sessions.

I was also aware that he had spoken to me with a certain guile and that he knew he was putting me in a most difficult situation. Certainly it felt a heinous thing to do to charge a patient for missing a session to be with his, literally dying, mother. I resisted the temptation to say, "Of course I won't charge you" and decided to sit tight, most of all because I felt that I had been trapped into an almost impossible situation.

I soon resolved that, heinous though it might be, I would charge him for that session and then I had to face the music. He was appalled by my callousness, greed, and insensitivity and over the next few weeks he would regularly convince me that I was indeed as he imagined me to be. He spoke to many of his relations and friends (some of whom were solicitors, one a specialist in fraud cases, he told me) who were equally affronted by his analyst's behaviour. Despite my, at times, great discomfort, I was sure that something very important was happening especially when the patient began to intersperse his complaints about me with reports of a recurring dream, or rather a recurring failure to have a dream. He had very rarely brought dreams to his analysis and this was more in the nature of a nightmare.

He was standing next to his mother's grave, out of the ground came decomposing arms that grasped him and pulled him into the coffin and next to her decomposing body.

At this point he would wake in a very anxious state. I noticed that as Mr B told me this he would squirm on the couch as though he felt that what he was describing was actually happening to him and he would cover his eyes in his attempts to shield himself from these images. He began to fear that they would enter his mind at any point of the day or night as indeed they increasingly did.

Tentatively I tried to link the arms that grasped and then pulled him into the grave with what he felt to be my grasping nature (the analysis took place in a part of England in which "grasping", as well as its usual meaning, has a very particular meaning of taking greedily for financial benefit). Mr B usually took such interpretations merely as my trying to deflect from the inarguable fact that the present situation had revealed me to be grasping and for a number of weeks the analysis floundered in this extremely uncomfortable atmosphere. He paid his bill, but I felt that the analysis might well have broken down at that point.

Over time, I noticed that Mr B's manner to me became slightly warmer, mainly, I thought, because he was becoming increasingly worried about the intrusive images that his nightmares created. At the same time my analytic interest in what was going on became greater than my personal discomfort at the thought of having charged him for that session. As my counter-transference altered in this way, one day with much difficulty, Mr B told me that at his mother's funeral, which had occurred on the Sunday following her death and hence before the session in which the storm about his fees broke, as the coffin had been lowered into the grave he had had the "terrible" thought: "I wonder what she left me in her will?". As he said this he shuddered, much as he did whenever he described his images of his mother's decomposing body. I took up with him how awful he felt about himself for having such a thought and he elaborated upon his feeling that everybody at the funeral would have been appalled at him were they to know about it. Interestingly, he later came to link the thought he'd had at the funeral with an intrusive image he had frequently experienced when giving his mother a drink in her last years, that of throwing the liquid into her face. This was part of a development in which he became more conscious of his aggression.

Mr B's nightmare images receded after the work described above and he was free of them from that time on. It was not the case that he came to thank me for making my stand about his fee; he continued to resent paying for missed sessions and the annual raising of his fee was always a painful process. However, it was consequently more possible for him to consider various aspects of his character, such as his greed and his wish to exert total control over his environment. Useful work was done in linking the above themes to the issue of his aging and, over the course of the next three years, he became more flexible and less persecuted in his relationship to time. His relationship with his partner matured further and he became far more tolerant of the normal physical imperfections of her middle-aged body which had bothered him greatly at the beginning of their relationship.

This period of analysis illustrates how a patient who was so overwhelmed by a piece of psychic reality (about his own acquisitiveness and aggression) that he could not face it, had to project it into other objects. He attempted to do this into the object of his mother's body, but this was not successful; he could not dream this, it became a nightmare that woke him and an image that haunted him. He projected it into his analyst, who then had to bear the very disturbing feelings that he was heinous, "grasping", concerned more for his pocket than his patient's welfare and that everyone who might come to know of this would abhor him. It was only after I had borne these feelings until they were detoxified and began to be a source of some professional interest, that the patient was able to admit to himself the thought that he too could be "grasping". Such acknowledgement of his own nature in turn detoxified his external world. Significantly, this also eventually led to a change in his feeling of paranoia about the passage of time, so that he no longer felt so persecuted by the limits it placed upon him.

Discussion

I have tried to show the importance of working through, in the counter-transference and its relationship to the patient's ability to synthesize, an issue to the point of being able to dream about it. In Bion's terms (1962) the patient is unable to apply alpha function to a beta element (for example a gut feeling of having been robbed of a fundamental right). The element is then felt to be fit only for evacuation via enactment, somatization or projection. The analyst also receives it as a beta element and his first reaction is to be rid of it. In the examples I have given this would involve ignoring the sense that one was being bored and robbed by Mr A, or in Mr B's case quickly saying: "In these extraordinary circumstances of course I won't charge you for the session".

If one does not rid oneself of the beta element, there follows a period of personal discomfort which can be very acute (as was mine with Mr B as he argued about the heinousness of my charging him.) Over time there is then some growing recognition that the nature of the discomfort has some analytic meaning connected to the patient. In such a situation this always seem to follow later and this illustrates Money-Kyrle's (1956) point that the analyst first experiences the counter-transference as primarily his own problem. Disentangling one's personal contribution to the counter-transference from the patient's is always a complicated matter. For example, in Mr B's case, for a number of weeks I was very uneasy about my conduct and slowly came to realize that I was anxious about the possibility that my commitment to maintaining the setting of the treatment, including the parameter of his paying for a missed session, was essentially a product of my personal need to feel professionally potent in a geographical location in which, at the time, I was the only psychoanalyst. Mr B, I am sure, took advantage of this uncertainty to promote the feeling in me that I was acting unethically. It was only after some working through in the counter-transference that I was able to own this personal dilemma and balance its importance against the clinical significance of the unfolding events. I could then take some satisfaction from this and feel relief that I had, after all, been properly concerned with maintaining a professional and psychoanalytical standard, as well as enacting a personal concern.

In order to be able to engage successfully in the process described above, the analyst must have available to him the capacity to consult with himself and to be able to tolerate waiting, in uncertainty, until he can think through what is going on, as my dream about Mr A demonstrates. This is not possible in very many cases and the analyst will unconsciously rid himself of discomforting beta elements before he has been able to apply a psychoanalytic function to them. In the early stages of one's clinical career, personal analysis and supervision can play some part in helping the development of the resources needed to do this work, although this is probably limited by the anxieties of being judged etc. However, because of the patient's tendency to pitch material beyond the analyst's capacity to understand, it is inevitable that throughout one's career there is always the possibility of evacuating rather than analysing the beta elements projected into one. This is in the nature of the activity of psychoanalysis. Some form of consultation with a colleague, whether it be in a formal supervision or a peer case discussion, can be crucial in such cases. In order for this to be helpful at the level I am describing, it is vital that the supervisory situation is one in which the narcissistic injury, which invariably seems to be produced by having one's blind spots pointed out, can be borne. This then allows a relatively frank description of the clinical material and a clearer conscious or unconscious communication about one's counter-transference.

It is clear that such dramatic manifestations of the process, as I have described, are not the constant work of analysis; there are long periods of time in which the analyst's equanimity may not be disturbed so unduly. However, it is likely to occur when two conditions are present as they were in my clinical examples. Firstly, each patient was bringing a most fundamental issue which had become part of the very fabric of their personality. Therefore, it was one which the analyst was likely to have adapted to unconsciously and was able to disregard until it produced sufficient discomfort over time (as with Mr A) or circumstances allowed it to erupt suddenly (as in Mr B's case). Secondly, I think it is highly relevant that both of these patients had early objects who seemed less than able to use their minds to try and empathize with their children's situation. For example, Mr A's mother believed he was throwing the ball at her and his father did not think that the children may not have known what his definition of eating wrongly was. I believe these were screen memories of early objects who could not be not be sufficiently mindful of their son. Although Mr B's mother was not so obviously disturbed, she was unable to empathize with her adult son when he was in great distress about his skin condition and, in the analysis, I gained a picture of a woman who had been very narcissistically invested in her son. Fonagy et al. (1991, 1993) have shown how important it is, for normal development, for the child's object to have the capacity to empathize with the child's experience and vicariously take the child's point of view. With patients who have been significantly deprived of an object with these capacities, I think it is much more likely that they will need to tax the analyst's capacity to bear disturbing projections; indeed a major part of their analysis may be to find, or create, an object who can function adequately as a container.

It is worthwhile distinguishing between the result of a process, for example an insight, and the process itself—in this case an analysis. Insights, in themselves, are relatively easy to gain, the text books are full of them, but, stripped of a process by which they are achieved, they are relatively useless. It is the process by which they are arrived at that gives them depth and a resonance of meaning which makes them valuable and can lead to change. It is a process in which one person is disturbed by the other and attempts to understand how this has happened and why it has had to happen. Some patients seem to know unconsciously that they need to experience such a process in order to get better. Hence, they pitch their material beyond the analyst's capacity to understand in order that their unthinkable and undreamable dilemmas can be metabolized from things that have to be compulsively repeated and/or projected to problems that can be felt and thought and dreamt about. In so doing, they demonstrate an ability to be aware of their object's capabilities and in this sense they show their regard and respect for the true nature of their object; the process I have described in this paper demonstrates a normal and healthy rather than a pathological use of projective identification. The patient's aim is to develop the capacities to think, to feel, and to dream.

References

Anzieu, D. (1985). The film of the dream. In: S. Flanders (Ed.), *The Dream Discourse Today*. London and New York: Routledge, 1993.

Bion, W. R. (1962). *Learning from Experience*. London: Heinemann.

Brenman Pick, I. (1985). Working through in the counter-transference. *International Journal of Psycho-Analysis, 66*: 157–167.

Carpy, D. V. (1989). Tolerating the countertransference: a mutative process. *International Journal of Psycho-Analysis, 70*: 287–295.

Fonagy, P., Steele, M., Moran, G. S., Steele, H., & Hignett, A. C. (1991). The capacity for understanding mental states: the reflective self in parent and child and its significance for security of attachment. *Inf. Ment. Health J., 13*: 200–216.

Fonagy, P., Steele, M., Moran, G. S., Steele, H., & Hignett, A. C. (1993). Measuring the ghost in the nursery: an empirical study of the relation between parents' mental representations of childhood experiences and their infants' security of attachment. *Journal of the American Psychoanalytical Association, 41*: 957–989.

Gammill, J. (1980). Some reflections on analytic listening and the dream screen. *International Journal of Psycho-Analysis, 61*: 375–383 [reprinted in *The Dream Discourse Today*, S. Flanders (Ed.). London and New York: Routledge, 1993].

Heimann, P. (1950). On counter-transference. *International Journal of Psycho-Analysis, 31*: 81–84.

Joseph, B. (1989). *Psychic Equilibrium and Psychic Change*. London and New York: Routledge.

Khan, M. M. R. (1962). Dream psychology and the evolution of the psychoanalytic situation. *International Journal of Psycho-Analysis, 43*: 21–31 [reprinted in *The Dream Discourse Today*, S. Flanders (Ed.). London and New York: Routledge, 1993].

Khan, M. M. R. (1972). The use and abuse of dream in psychic experience. In: *The Privacy of the Self*. London: Hogarth Press, 1974 [reprinted in *The Dream Discourse Today*, S. Flanders (Ed.). London and New York: Routledge, 1993].

Money-Kyrle, R. (1956) Normal countertransference and some of its deviations. *International Journal of Psycho-Analysis, 37*: 360–366 [reprinted in *Melanie Klein Today, Volume 2, Mainly Practice*, E. Bott Spillius (Ed.). London and New York: Routledge, 1988].

Lewin, B. (1946). Sleep, the mouth and the dream screen. *Psychoanalytic Quarterly, 15*: 419–434.

Lewin, B. (1953). Reconsideration of the dream screen. *Psychoanalytic Quarterly, 22*: 174–199.

Lewin, B. (1955). Dream psychology and the analytic situation. *Psychoanalytic Quarterly, 24*: 169–199.

Sandler, J. (1976). Counter-transference and role responsiveness. *International Review of Psychoanalysis, 3*: 43–47.

Segal, H. (1981). The function of dreams. In: J. S. Grotstein (Ed.), *Do I Dare Disturb the Universe?* Beverley Hills, CA: Caeswa Press [reprinted in *The Dream Discourse Today*, S. Flanders (Ed.). London and New York: Routledge, 1993].

Stewart, H. (1973). The experiencing of the dream and the transference. *International Journal of Psycho-Analysis, 54*: 345–349 [reprinted in *The Dream Discourse Today*, S. Flanders (Ed.). London and New York: Routledge, 1993].

CHAPTER THREE

The dream space, the analytic situation and the eating disorder: clinging to the concrete

Sarah Flanders

P atients frequently bring to the analytic situation objections to the boundaries and limitations of that space, their argument with the fundamentally symbolic nature of the psychoanalytic situation. The argument is particularly intense in those patients who come to the analytic situation still "clinging to the concrete", still holding on firmly to the belief in magical, omnipotent solutions, without which anxiety leads too readily to an experience of helplessness (Freud, 1926). Their struggle with the analytic space, and the confusion provoked by its demand on symbolic capacities, will find expression in their idiosyncratic use of the dream. Within that context, Masud Khan, in particular, has drawn attention to the similarities between the dreamer's capacity to have a "useful" or "good dream", one capable of processing symbolically the ego's *awakened* (Lewin, 1955) wishes and fears, and Ernst Kris's classical conceptualization of the "good analytic hour". He reminds us of the many emotional achievements implicit in these capacities. Both the "good dream" and the "good analytic hour", for example, require a trust in a benign regression, an ability to suspend involvement with external reality, a capacity for symbolic satisfaction, all complex developments born out of the object relationships which are their foundation (Khan, 1962). Later, Khan went on to link the capacity to use a dream creatively within the psychoanalytic situation to Winnicott's conceptualization of play, relating the "dream space" to "transitional space", the field of play in which the child and then the adult learns to express and explore, symbolically, his wishes and fears. Winnicott's exploration of the child's complex developmental achievement in acquiring symbolic capacity, informs our understanding and recognition of its failure, or breakdown, within the facilitating, but also demanding, environment of the psychoanalytic situation (Winnicott, 1971).

I will use the unfolding analysis of a young woman with an eating disorder to illustrate the profound anxieties awakened by the demands of the analytic situation, both its boundaries and its intimacy, and disclose those tensions illustrated in significant dreams. I will show the relationship between her eating disorder and her difficulty in making use of the analytic situation, her clinging to the concrete in preference to the more problematic metabolization of complex and confusing emotions, and then show this tension disclosed in some of her dreams, as they appeared at significant moments. The opposite emotional catastrophes of invasion and abandonment, *awakened* by the power of the transference and linked to the analytic activities of interpretation within a context of a firm psychoanalytic boundary, provoke explosive anxieties and frustrations which compel the patient to use an eating disorder: her omnipotent defence. It is her triumphant way of controlling and combating the effects of the psychoanalytic understanding she both seeks and dreads. The movement in this analysis, for many years, will be constantly back and forth, between the good work of dream, symbolic work, thinking, emotional growth, and its negation, often made real in the concrete undoing of the eating binge. The binge, I understand as a product of the temporary breakdown of the symbolic capacities, the loss of safety in the symbolic activity, which becomes a bad experience, one that needs to be defended against, triumphed over, and attacked. My understanding of the breakdown of the symbolic process, depends on Bion's conceptualization of containment and its failures, and Hannah Segal's elaboration of these failures as they are specifically disclosed in the patient's relationship to dreaming, particularly her understanding of symbolic equation. Using Bion's notion of the contact barrier (Bion, 1962), conceptualized, like Lewin's dream screen and Winnicott's transitional space, as an internalization and development of maternal care and handling, Segal describes the failure of that capacity in the mind to bind symbolically the information coming from outside and inside. The failure eventuates in a foreclosure of the mind, and in concrete manifestations, such as the symptomatology of the patient, Ms X.

Ms X was referred for treatment in her late twenties, having been encouraged by her boyfriend to get psychotherapeutic help. She had recently moved into his small flat, and they were not having a happy time. She could feel the danger of repeating a sadomasochistic, eventually violent sexual relationship of the past, and she feared that her present partner, himself in intensive psychotherapy for a number of years following a serious breakdown, would finish with her if the relationship took this turn. She acknowledged, though not quite directly, that she did not know how to have pleasure that did not bring violent anxieties along with it. I did not know at this initial meeting that she had already begun to gain the weight she had lost after she had finally extricated herself from the relationship that had become so mutually abusive, though she observed at our first meeting that all the women in the family, her mother, and her spinster sister, eleven years her senior, had a problem with food. As an adolescent, this intelligent and pretty young woman had kept her weight low enough not to have regular periods, disclosing the determined control of which she was capable, the concrete solutions on which she was reliant, and the degree of anxiety about becoming an adult and sexual woman which marked her adolescence. She wanted help with this anxiety, which was now disturbing her with fresh intensity. She had long ago consciously rejected her sister's solution—the sister who had announced to her at an impressionable age, when the elder was seventeen and the patient six, that she would never have a boyfriend, she would never be kissed. The sister has remained true to her word, carving for herself a very successful professional career, establishing an emotional equilibrium at the expense of a sexual life. The extremity of her sister's situation represents a disturbing conundrum for Ms X, who perceives her as the "good" daughter in the eyes of her parents, a place she would like to occupy, even though she rejects the conditions, as she perceives them, and regards her sister's renunciation as a profound and painful price to pay for parental approval and emotional stability.

When she came into treatment, in her late twenties, Ms X described herself as still bound to her own mother, who claimed to know everything about her, to be just like her, and who demonstrated her closeness to her well into her adolescence, for example, by meeting her every day without fail on her way home from school, until the patient went off to university. Once there Ms X stopped being anorexic and, after her first sexual relationship, discovered in bingeing a more active method of displacing and controlling anxiety. Unlike her sister, she had claimed a sexual life, and she had concurrently moved from anorexic defences to bingeing, though never to vomiting.

Moreover, Ms X felt aware that the "special" relationship she had in relation to her mother partly facilitated her entering sexual life. Her mother, in affectionately calling her "horrible"—often presented by the patient as contrary to the "good" big sister—proffered a protective shield, which in some measure saved her youngest daughter's right to pleasure, while linking it in her mind with a rather caricatured image of badness that haunted and delimited her determined pursuit of happiness.

The complexity of this "badness", which includes features of destructive narcissism (Rosenfeld, 1971) as well as the salvation of her sexual life, even the salvation of life itself, has been one of the very difficult knots in her psyche to untie, and her ferocious loyalty to the confusion bound up with "badness", one of the underlying difficulties in helping her to develop. At the time of referral, she was driving her partner crazy, unable to bear his turning his attention away from her, experiencing the most ordinary separation as abandonment and simultaneous confirmation of the "badness" which, according to the mother/daughter mythology, only her mother, not her father, and probably no man could enduringly love.

To add to the paradox, her "badness" was associated with the actual fact of maturation, not only the bad periods, which she kept at bay in adolescence, but the maturing out of infancy which she associated with being dropped from her father's affections. Her memory has never wavered from a conviction that he radically lost interest in his beautiful baby daughter when she reached the age of six or seven, roughly the time at which her mother and she became inseparably bound up, also the time at which her own mother's aged and ill mother, who lived in the home, died. A cloud of deadly depression hangs over the bond with her mother, while an equation of separation and death is often implicit in the anxiety she has brought to treatment. From the very beginning, she articulated the feeling that embarking on psychotherapy was a betrayal of her bond with her mother; she was convinced she was really hurting her, and she voiced early on the adolescent conviction that if she were really to own her separation from her mother, she would kill her mother. Gaining weight saved her from feeling she had got away: they were both overweight; the same. The concrete solution obviated the need for mental work. It constituted a triumph over the conditions of reality, over the losses which are the crucial building blocks of emotional growth and the symbolic functioning, which is its complement and compensation. It also enacted a masochistic reproach to both the hard working analyst and the hard working patient.

The analytic boundaries, the eating disorder, and the dream

In the beginning, the analytical boundaries which Ms X experienced as cruel in the extreme, became a central and dominant preoccupation. Like many patients who have had acute difficulties in owning their own separateness, she complained of feeling totally devastated by the end of the session, describing a radical temperature drop, for example, on leaving the consulting room. In the beginning, the hell of exclusion was mitigated by a vacancy becoming available, then another. My ability to increase the frequency of her sessions, (initially she came twice a week), proved useful, inasmuch as she needed full analysis, but this also delayed the full crisis of an encounter with actual limits, and fitted in too neatly with demand for concrete gratification; a session instead of a cake.

Ms X brought her first dream after coming four times per week for three weeks, that is, after entering analysis, and then being able to have consecutive sessions. The value of continuity has long been a cornerstone in support of psychoanalysis. It is an aspect of the safety of the psychoanalytic session for the patient, who is not left too long with potentially unbearable anxiety. For the analytic study of the patient's mental processes, continuity provides a laboratory best able to disclose the unconscious processes, the mental metabolization of the day before, the day's residue, which includes the psychoanalytic hour. A session supported by preceding and succeeding sessions provides a window most likely to disclose, often through the dream of the night before, the patient's own experience of the "awakening" of the analysis (Lewin, 1955; Khan, 1962).

> In the chaos of controlling her anxiety in the first ten months of treatment, Ms X had gained two stone, a fact I failed to register until the patient came to a session upset by a confrontational GP who told her to lose ten kilos or she would not renew her birth control pill prescription. This encounter with the GP preceded the first dream. On the day before the dream, she had dieted, but before bed she ate a bowl of cereal and a tin of beans, her sleeping draught, her baby-like method of quieting the anxiety and rage associated with the GP's intrusion, and my recurrent abandonment. Her dream:

> *She came to a session, but arrived at a different house. There is a large garden and about fifty people milling around. These are my patients. She cannot have a Monday session. She knocks on windows with a rock, angry and upset. There is an older man and a younger woman who want to help her. They seem to be extensions of my power and me.*

> She was able to think about the dream, and quickly agreed that the overt anger, the knocking with a rock, found expression in the dream, as it does not in her sessions. She associated to the older man and younger woman, her female GP and her boyfriend, perhaps also his analyst. Grievances about deprivation continued the theme of "cannot haves": her boyfriend had asked her to move out of his flat, her boyfriend had more sessions than she did, he didn't have to leave work, his therapist told him he was "the best" when he applied for a job, I would never do as much, her boyfriend even had sessions on the telephone. Threaded through the litany of complaints was recognition of an achievement over the past months. In her new flat she could sometimes bear, though certainly not enjoy, being in a separate room from her boyfriend. She no longer compulsively involved herself in the constant touching which she

thinks drove her partner crazy when they lived together in his smaller flat. In some way, she was being helped to stay in the sexual relationship, to turn some of her anxiety to the hated depriving analyst, rather than torturing the boyfriend for being other and therefore outside her control.

Against the rather grim observation of the bleakly bearable separateness came an ambiguous association to her mother, superior and dangerous, who "knows everything", probably even the fact of her being in therapy, even though she had not told her anything of it. I took her mother's superiority to mean the mother who, *a priori*, knows everything, not like the analyst, with whom she needed to work. Fundamentally, this was an interpretation aimed at her disappointment in not having the narcissistic support of an alliance with an omnipotent analyst, the loss she struggled with bitterly. The interpretation aimed to meet the opposite dread, the fear of the all-knowing analyst, a dread which would materialize more intensely in the future. She surprised me with an unexpected link to toilet training, one associatively relevant to the troubled state she found herself in: She said that she'd been told she was toilet trained before the age of one, and added, with a cryptic mixture of dismay and pride, before the "age of awareness". I understood her to be describing compliance, the dangers of being a patient having to fit in with whatever sessions I deigned to offer, without understanding the process of which she is told she has the need, for which she feels need, but in which she is not an equal partner. In connection to the toilet training, I said that she did not expect her needs to be attended to, nor to experience herself held, a word I knew was full of ambiguous possibilities, which I hoped would link with the deep anxieties of both abandonment and intrusion to which she was alluding in her various associations. She responded that, if as an infant she was held much, she thought it was by her father. I noted that her father was the one whom she described as setting limits, the limits she associated with me, the finality of the ending of the sessions, like a cliff, an unbearable boundary, one which left her feeling bad.

At the time I understood this dream to mark a level of increased interest in and concern with an inner world even as the preoccupation remained so focused on my hated boundaries and me. Having conceived the limits of concrete gratification from me, although she had not quite at this time achieved the limit, which is coming five times per week, she had begun to realize, in a very conflicted way, the actual limits as well as the symbolic possibilities of the psychoanalytic situation. She had begun the work, which would carry on for most of this analysis. The experience of a boundary within a context, which promises and indeed delivers an experience of continuity, contributes to the development of the symbolic capacities attributed to what Bion calls the "contact barrier" or, in another, more embodied conceptualization, the ego skin of Anzieu (1989), as well as the dream screen of Lewin. The contact barrier, conceived by Bion, is built up out of the transformation of inchoate infantile experience through the work of maternal containment. It contributes to the differentiation of conscious and unconscious thought, to the establishment and maintenance of Khan's "dream space" (1974). Ms X's rage has found a dwelling place, in the dream, where it is bound; (de Moncheaux, 1978; Pontalis, 1974) and in keeping with a rigidity which will shift very slowly, where it remains. This patient never raised her voice in my presence, never threatened my pane of glass, and she remained careful and modulated in the sessions. It would be a very long time before the anger found direct expression in a session. Her own concrete contribution to producing a good enough sleep to produce her dream of bearable deprivation, which had been one bowl of cereal and one tin of beans, marks the limits of her faith in the symbolic, or her tolerance of needing or valuing my understanding, or her belief in my tolerating a rage which she thinks no one can bear.

The food, unlike my understanding or concern, is finally under her control, in her possession, concretely in her grasp, in her mouth, in her stomach and does not retaliate or punish, until it confirms her shittiness masochistically. Much later, when she is in touch with her fury at her mother for preferring sleeping babies, for having given birth to her under general anaesthetic, for having been ill during her first months, she will clarify the great dread of her own emotional life which is awakened in the analytic situation, provoked by the analytic limitations and controlled by the displacement onto food. In this dream she has been able to acknowledge the rage at feeling thwarted by my not being one hundred per cent available. At this time, this painful realization reflected the dominating and humiliating pain of her life, as her boyfriend had asked her, in the interests of preserving their relationship, to move out of his tiny flat. Her great difficulty in tolerating the fact of their separateness, her great difficulty in coming together and then separating, dominated her intimate relations, and had done so since she actually embarked on the intimate relations she was determined to have when she left home as an adolescent. This had been the crux of her young adulthood, and the motivation for the bingeing, which had replaced the anorexic defence when she entered sexual life.

The dream space invaded

The tension in the analysis eventually shifted away from the attack on my limits, my separateness, yielding to a more paranoid anxiety about my intrusion, an anxiety already disclosed in the associations to the first dream. These anxieties too had been controlled by the anorexic defence in adolescence, and were now expressed in the defiant relationship to food, an expression of omnipotence in relation to an object stripped of its capacity to feel or to think. Inasmuch as I had made inroads into her mental life, as manifested by the dream, I became the dangerous internal invader. To the extent that the analysis came between her and her conviction of being the same as and bound to her mother, it awakened her immense anxiety and guilt about separating from her mother. This anxiety became manifest in pressurized torment that she would have to have a hysterectomy, as her mother had in the second year of Ms X's analysis. (Ms X, who consciously hated her mother's relation to physical medicine, perceived by Ms X as hypochon-driacal, nevertheless had, in late adolescence, the same surgical procedure shortly after her mother, in an unconscious identification which confirmed for Ms X her mother's potent and witch like magic, rather than the power of her unconscious identification.) Shortly after her mother's hysterectomy, she herself became racked with a pain that both she and I believed to be entirely psychological until it began to have an insistence that signified a real danger. Finally, it would be diagnosed as the product of an infected appendix that did indeed threaten her ovaries, requiring surgery. The necessity of the operation displaced her paranoid hatred of the intrusive aspect of the analysis onto the real intrusions of medical practice. Boundaries were again a dominant issue, both of the body, and of the mind. The intrusions by interpretation into the inner world and its precarious equilibrium were made concrete in the actual intrusions by doctors, who eventually cut into her body, and took out the infected part.

A series of dreams from the next period of her analysis marks the process of the analytical evolution, more clearly focused on the problematic anxiety of her analyst getting inside her rather than keeping her on the outside. This series bears witness, I think, to her struggle to trust in the analytic situation, and to a corresponding access to a dream space. In particular her argument is with the *confusion* she associated with complex emotions, the recognition of which is the business of the analytic process. She brought these three dreams in a sequence, some weeks after she had come back to analysis following the appendectomy, which had terrified her.

Her first dream:

She and her boyfriend are at the beach, at the water's edge. There is a black ship at sea, and off it floats a little white boat. There is a battle between those in the sea and those in the boat. [The battle was obscure to me, even when I asked her about it.] She and he go to the beach house, which is bleak inside. It looks as if the outline of a head is under the sheets on a bed. She takes her boyfriend away to a hotel, which is lit up and full of people.

She associates the bleak beach house with his family, which she thinks of as sterile and depriving and the warm hotel with herself and her family, which is also "bad". This badness is also associated with the bigger black boat.

Her second dream:

She dreams of being bathed, soothed but not interfered with, clean, no longer dirty.

Her third dream:

She dreams she is washing her hair. There are big bugs falling out of it. There is a very concrete feeling to this last dream; I can almost hear the bugs making contact with the floor as she speaks.

This interesting series of dreams was paradoxically presented as the patient complained of an emotional state of feeling isolated, untouchable, unreachable, a state that on this day upset her; it was not presented as desirable, safely out of reach. The dreams convey some good spaces: particularly the bath, more problematically the hotel: and some clearly frightening objects: the bugs, the head under the sheets. Ms X was unusually generous in her associations, although there were some significant blanks, notably the nature of the fight or battle, which was very obscure, and the head under the sheets remained a mystery, containing a powerful atmosphere of dread. Material from previous sessions, previous interpretations of mine relating to a black and white view of the world, had entered into the first dream, including the problematic ambiguity of her "badness". The black boat was associated with her "bad" family, but so was the hotel, which seemed to promise warmth, pleasure, and welcome. Leading her boyfriend to the hotel, a container of something lively, implied access to something good which she could also give, something inside her which she could use. She acknowledged this movement in the dream, which at this point marked some small change in her feelings about herself. There is, therefore, in this first dream, an unravelling of some hardened convictions; they include a belief that her own parents were too dangerously destructive to be encountered, even psychologically encountered, for fear of a psychic collapse, a loss of the rigid and paranoid structures which sustained her capacity to be separate, to have a sexual relationship. She was frightened of a physical and emotional contamination of dire consequence.

In relation to the second dream, we had observed the feeling of harmonious contact, the feeling held, soothed, warmed though not touched, in a bath which also, she noted, meant she was no longer dirty. Being bathed is one way of soothing the body and physically restoring an equilibrium that is almost as close as possible to the intrauterine, narcissistic state to which Freud (1916) suggested we try to return at night, in our sleep. Being bathed is the image Didier Anzieu returns to frequently when he writes of the repair or restoration of the body ego, the ego skin, a repair which he conceived the ego returning to nightly in dreams (Anzieu, 1989). In this dream, Ms X clearly brings in the anguished problematic of bad feelings confused with dirt, complexity confused with con-tamination, and the body as container and field on which this confusion is enacted. As may be expected of anyone with an eating disorder, Ms X struggled with great torment in relation to a body she tried hard not to hate, but which she associated with her convictions of her fathers rejection of her and her mother's self loathing.

So far, I felt that she had let me get alongside her to think about her dreams in a creative way, and she herself was involved in thinking and associating in a way that seemed to belie the isolated state of mind of which she complained. However, when I hazarded a view regarding the bugs in the third dream, she pushed me away quite vehemently.

> I said to her, late in what seemed to be the "good analytic hour" fostered by the bringing of "good dreams" for analytic work, that along with a willingness to explore, she was actually feeling like she wanted to be rid of the thoughts which made her seem bad, or even at risk of being mad, that she was disturbed by bringing her thoughts more openly to the session. She said to me very firmly "no", less it seemed to me to the content of what I was saying, but more to my intrusiveness, myself experienced as a disorganizing function (Williams, 1997). There was no elaboration on this "no", it was pushed up as a protective shield. I felt myself intruder, even potential abuser, and I felt aware of the sensitive reality of her head being the part of her so close to me in reality in the consulting room.

At the time, I was deeply impressed by the combination of unprecedented cooperation in thinking about the first and second dream, and unprecedented conflict with me, in the outspoken "no entry" (Williams, 1997) defence so firmly erected against me, when I interpreted the concreteness of the final dream. I posited to myself that if she could disclose such a dream to me, and yet also say no to my interpretation as it impinged on her intrusively, perhaps she would be able to allow greater contact with her inner world, her rigidly controlled inner objects and would likewise be more available to what I had to say. I thought she might not feel so endangered of helplessly submitting to either the dangerous internal objects, or me as their representative, and in this submission, lose the prospect of a separate and sexual identity—one of the terrors of her emotional life. I thought, in this session, of Spitz's study of the developmental function of negation, (Spitz, 1957) the acquisition of the toddler, and related it to her history, as I conceived it, of a toddler much projected into by the family, particularly the mother, father, and pubertal sister. Such thinking on my part was seeking the developmental positives in what was without doubt a sample of concrete thinking, an expulsive process (Segal, 1980), a radical undoing of integration or working through. Washing big bugs out of her hair is her way of keeping to an unambiguous, concrete understanding of good and bad, turning complex and frightening feelings and thoughts to small things which can be omnipotently controlled, washed out. There is a foreclosure in her "bugs", and a negation of the evolution, the change or development through understanding with which I continued to bug her.

It is notable that these dreams and this open "no" to me, which I, as analyst, thought marked a capacity to reinforce a boundary, therefore a potential to more safely suspend her boundaries, potentially facilitating the "regression in the service of the ego" which marks the "good analytic hour" (Kris, 1952, 1956) left her feeling something so miserably different: isolated, exposed, vulnerable, perhaps skinless. I saw, particularly in her first dream and most importantly, in her associations to it, a capacity to use her experience of feeling loved in a good way. She was able to acknowledge that she had, for example, been raised in an atmosphere of concern and warmth, however much that atmosphere was marked by her fathers rigid obsessionality and her mother's hypochondriacal possessiveness, a context of great anxiety, and much symptomatic structuring of powerful dreads. But Ms X did not share in my optimistic understanding of her capacity to hold inside of herself these more complex and I think more realistic conceptualizations. That session was followed by abject terror of change, a sense that analysis was too difficult; she could not pursue it without becoming hopelessly contaminated and confused. Her deep ambivalence about the analytic process, a process which has found its way into her dreams, here ended on a strongly repudiating note, the denigrated and concretized image of the bad thoughts analysis is experienced as putting into her.

The struggle continues

This analysis nonetheless continued. Ms X was committed to her emotional growth despite the overwhelming anxiety which accompanied it. Slowly, she was able to develop a more complex and sustainable relation to the inner objects she nonetheless continued to dread. When an experience of contamination, or the bleakness of emotional impoverishment, or an intolerable rage overwhelmed her, she would binge. (This bingeing never resulted in vomiting, nor did Ms X ever, since entering treatment, abuse or even use any potentially destructive or "bad" substances, except insofar as chocolate or crisps could be described as bad.) The bingeing became confined to weekends, almost ritualized around the time that her boyfriend would have a weekend session with his therapist, something I did not offer. This compulsive and driven eating was almost always associated with a reproach for my absence, my not being present for her in the hour of the weekend when she needed me to help her contain the envy and humiliation of not getting what her boyfriend got, in short, my making her feel bad.

For a number of years the psychic movement in and, significantly, between sessions moved along the lines made clear in the sequence of dreams reported: understanding would be followed by a radical undoing of the integration experienced by Ms X as dangerous, exposing, and contaminating. Her somewhat triumphant negation of psychoanalytic work would be accompanied by an almost palpable masochism, which was often visibly apparent in an abject appearance, her clothing ragged and self denigrating rather than bohemian chic, a certain sign that a binge had taken place. Sometimes the dangerous understanding was lost to the mind and sent into her body, which would develop some remarkable and real, psychosomatic, but not hypochondriacal, physical symptom. All of Ms X's physical symptoms carried historical and symbolic significance; all, she could acknowledge, contained meaning which the analysis could elaborate; most also carried insistent physical impact which required the medical intervention Ms X deplored and dreaded. Just as I was kept at a distance and controlled by the eating disorder, so I, or we, failed in words to contain the violent antagonisms which erupted in the body. The violent eruption of physical symptoms, the most serious being the appendicitis which preceded the previous set of dreams, delineated the boundary of my potency, the limits of analytic insight. Ms X produced dreams, intermittently, but the associations to those dreams were often minimal, cryptic, keeping me out. I believe there is a correspondence here between the dream space and

Ms X's experience of her bodily boundaries; the shallow or truncated symbolical elaboration of the body is reflected in the need to keep me out of the dream space, as was illustrated in the response to my interpretation of the last dream in the sequence previously discussed.

The extent to which the psychoanalytic situation was not in Ms X's control was made more real when, in the fourth year of the analysis, I moved consulting rooms, something which she resented bitterly, although it marked a significant turning point in the analysis. This proof that I was not in her control, shook what safe foundations we had managed to establish, and the extremely punishing sessions which surrounded this dreaded event are testament to the extreme anxiety with which Ms X struggled. It no doubt also discloses the extent to which the anxiety driven need to feel in control had become identified with the unchanging parameters of the psychoanalytic situation. At the news that I would be working from a new consulting room, she experienced herself torn away from those parameters, ripped from the boundaries which had become merged with her own, the imaginary baby ripped from the body of the mother/analyst. Day in and day out prior to this move Ms X came to her sessions with a grim furious grievance, and a conviction that this change, which I had arrived at without consulting her, constituted a profound and damaging betrayal which put all her trust in jeopardy, and awakened the hatred which made her feel mad and bad.

The actual fact of the move was, when accomplished, most creative for Ms X. To her amazement, her analysis continued and she was able to accommodate the change. There was, therefore, a continuity of a process which she came to recognize as a symbolic process, and a simultaneous strengthening of the living relationship with me. The room changed, the procedure continued, a structure held, I remained the same, the space for thinking, the symbolic space, survived her attacks. In her relief at the continuation of the analysis, she herself initiated questions provoked by her own conscious awakening to an emotional appreciation of the difference between her phantasy and reality and the symbolic space in which the two are mediated. Having survived this move, which she had tenaciously fought as a symbolic equation (Segal, 1980) of parental abandonment (both a maternal abandonment and most, consciously, a repetition of her father's withdrawal from her as she moved from infancy into childhood), she woke up, as it were to find that it *represented* such an abandonment, but it was not a raw repetition. This was a mutative moment in her analysis, or became one, though not before I experienced myself as her executioner. The battle she fought with me was, for her, a life and death battle, the anxiety at the heart of it a struggle for survival. And her relief, to discover that the terms of the struggle were a delusion, was not unqualified. Reflecting on the painful learning from experience, she articulated, to my surprise, that there is a loss of control when the separation of symbol and symbolized is acknowledged, and it seemed too much to lose.

There was, nonetheless, on an unconscious level, a release from some of the burdens which omnipotence weighed on her. She was able to grieve for some real sadness that she could experience and momentarily acknowledge as beyond her control, beyond also the omnipotent control she had associated with the idealized parents of her childhood. She grieved for a real damaged baby, born recently in her extended family, a beautiful boy who would never develop, and she grieved again for the cousin who had briefly graced her adolescence and then been killed in an accident. She had suddenly a very strong realization of the extent to which she had been in conflict with her development, trying to remain her mother's and her father's permanent baby and still not pay the price paid by her celibate sister, of never entering the world of adult sexuality. This awareness of a battle against change, against development, fundamentally against the reality of the body's timebound and changing existence, is a familiar theme amongst eating disordered patients, and the argument is with the reality of development, the losses it entails, the demands of internalization, and the changing relationship to the parents of childhood. The determinedly held illusion of control struck her forcibly: she could not believe, she said, again to my surprise, how powerfully she had attacked the truth. The full tragedy of a permanently damaged development confronted her attention, and I did not have to work hard to enlarge her realization of the damage she could do to her own development, through her terror of the inevitable changes which are the result of living in time.

She betrayed a feeling of frustration, a wish for more from me, rather than simply suffering my interpretations.

She came to a session feeling, she said, curiously, hungry, in which it was my understanding that she was asking for more from me, she was hungry for food for thought. She brought a dream which I believe discloses an increase in a willingness to trust in the analytic situation and process, which was supported by the survival of her analytic sessions.

She is swimming. She is leading a group in choppy, turbulent water. They are going out, further, into the ocean, yet when she puts her feet down, she can touch.

Though the dream has the quality again of the magical baby she still aspired to be, it also has bottom, a basis, which I interpreted as the firm boundaries of the analytic situation she had come to believe in. The anxiety about abandonment, or annihilation, the infinity of terrors which plague her are bound by the fact that she can "touch". She has acquired a more reliable dream space, as well as a more reliable transitional or framed space in the psychoanalytic consulting room with me. This dream has resonance with the true history of her swimming, an activity which she has enjoyed since she learned to swim in the pool built in the garden of her childhood home by her father, when she was approaching puberty. It was a pool in which she could touch the bottom, a pool in which she taught herself to swim. In and around this pool, where she often swam and sunbathed alone, she had been befriended by a relative regarded as the golden youth of the extended family, and his choosing her to be his friend marked a precious turning point as well as a painfully lost period of her life; this beloved and gratefully appreciated youth (already referred to in this paper, and a recurrent figure in her analytic narrative) was tragically killed in an accident a few years after he befriended Ms X. This loss represented a punishing trauma to Ms X, and the bleakness of her adolescence owes something to her unbearable anxiety and guilt about this boy's death. However, her father's provision of a place of warmth, protection, pleasure, remained in her mind a benign and generative, if largely latent patriarchal provision, and at this point in her analysis, it gained some weight in her psychic structure.

This analysis continues. The omnipotent and panic driven baby inside Ms X is not in total control and she has been able to use creatively much of what she has allowed herself to learn. In the months following this dream, she taught her boyfriend to swim. She would, in one year's time, become pregnant with her first child, sell her flat, and move in with her boyfriend. All of this would sorely tax her capacity to think, to bear the ambivalence she found so confusing, and the guilt which accompanied so much of her joy. There would be much greater demand on her to integrate feeling, and corresponding recourse to her concrete defence, but except in the most paranoid phases of pregnancy, she retained a capacity to dream, and to think about her dreams.

References

Anzieu, D. (1989). *The Skin Ego*. London: Yale.

Bion, W. (1962). *Learning from Experience*. London: Heinemann [reprinted in paperback, Maresfield Reprints, London: Karnac Books, 1984].

de Monchaux, C. (1978). Dreaming and the organizing function of the ego. *International Journal of the Psycho-Analytic Association*, *59* [reprinted in *The Dream Discourse Today*, Sara Flanders (Ed.). London: Routledge, 1993].

Freud, S. (1916). *Introductory Lectures on Psychoanalysis, Standard Edition of the Complete Psychological Works of Sigmund Freud. S.E., 15*. London: Hogarth Press, 1950–1970.

Freud, S. (1926). *Inhibitions, Symptoms and Anxiety. S.E., 20*. London: Hogarth Press.

Green, A. (1998). The primordial mind and the work of the negative. *International Journal of the Psycho-Analytic Association*, 649–665.

Khan, (1962). Dream psychology and the evolution of the psycho-analytic situation. *International Journal of the Psycho-Analytic Association*, *43* [reprinted in *The Dream Discourse Today*, S. Flanders (Ed.), New Library of Psychoanalysis. London: Routledge, 1993].

Khan, (1974). The use and abuse of dream in psychic experience. In: *The Privacy of the Self*. London: Hogarth [reprinted in *The Dream Discourse Today*, S. Flanders (Ed.). London: Routledge, 1993].

Kris, E. (1952). *Psychoanalytic Explorations in Art*. New York: International Universities Press.

Kris, E. (1956). On some vicissitudes of insight in psychoanalysis. *International Journal of the Psycho-Analytic Association*, *37*: 445–455.

Lewin, B. (1946). Sleep, the mouth and the dream screen. *The Psychoanalytic Quarterly*, *15*: 419–434.

Lewin, B. (1955). Dream psychology and the analytic situation. *The Psychoanalytic Quarterly*, 25: 169–199.

Pontalis, J.-B. (1974). The dream as an object. *International Review of Psychoanalysis* [reprinted in *The Dream Discourse Today*, Sara Flanders (Ed.). London: Routledge, 1993].

Rosenfeld, H. (1971). A clinical approach to the psychoanalytical theory of the life and death instincts. *International Journal of the Psycho-Analytic Association*, 52: 169–178.

Segal, H. (1980) The function of dreams. In: *The Work of Hannah Segal* [reprinted in *The Dream Discourse Today*, S. Flanders (Ed.), New Library of Psychoanalysis. London: Routledge, 1993].

Spitz, R. (1957). *No and Yes: On The Genesis of Human Communication*. New York: International Universities Press.

Williams, G. (1997) Reflections on some dynamics of eating disorders: "no entry" defences and foreign bodies. *International Journal of the Psycho-Analytic Association*, 78: 927–941.

CHAPTER FOUR

Dreams, symbolic impoverishment, and the question of the other

Gregorio Kohon

I

The knowledge with which psychoanalytic enterprise is concerned refers to a truth that is always unwelcome. It is unwelcome mainly because it is unconscious and does not depend on the will, or on the wishes of the subject. Patient and analyst get involved in a rather peculiar dialogue, in which both hope to be able to investigate and to question the symptom, the complaints, or the patient's predicament. At any event, the truth about the patient will appear where it is least expected. In this sense, it will surprise the analyst as much as the patient. The patient is invited to feel free to think and speak without inhibitions—no limitations are imposed upon him by the analyst. Whatever comes to mind can be thought and said, and there is a more or less explicit agreement established between patient and analyst that certain feelings and fantasies will not be put into action. Murderous feelings or violent fantasies, for example, will be dreamt or uttered, not realized in action.

It is never quite straightforward. Resistance will make its appearance, and verbalization sooner or later will be replaced by

acting out. Within the confines of this presentation, I use the term
acting out in a specific, technical way. The criteria to define certain
actions as acting out are: (1) the link of the action to the transference;
(2) the nature of the action (whether it attacks the setting, or the
possibility for insight: cf. Etchegoyen, 1986); and (3) the motivation
behind the action (the unconscious conflict). If we do not keep to
these criteria, then almost any behaviour that is disruptive to the
treatment could be seen as "acting out". At one time in psychoanalytic circles, the term was in fact used loosely and descriptively.
This only served the analyst's counter-transference: what analysts
might not have liked about the patient's behaviour, they called
"acting out". Nowadays, analysts seem to concentrate more on the
positive aspects of acting out, and it has come to be considered—at
least potentially—as a source of communication, perhaps at times
the only way that a patient can communicate something to the
analyst (Balint, 1954; Limentani, 1966). New concepts like enactments, re-enactments, and actualization in the transference have
emerged to become themes of great interest in the psychoanalytic
literature.

Enactment can be seen as the externalization (i.e. in action) in the
transference relationship of what the subject is experiencing in his
internal world. Sometimes it consists of an actualization in the
analytic situation of a transferential wish, which has been described
by Joseph Sandler as role-responsiveness (Sandler, 1976). An earlier
concept to Sandler's was Leon Grinberg's projective counter-
identification, which described how the analyst is "dragged" into
playing a role that the patient "forces" upon him through
pathological projective identification (Grinberg, 1956, 1957, 1963).
A more specific and dramatic form of enactment is constituted by
the re-enactment (or reliving) of an early traumatic experience in the
analytic relationship. At the same time, in contemporary psychoanalytic writings there has also been a growing interest in the
analyst's own contributions to the enactments and re-enactments
through the counter-transference.

I would like to suggest that both concepts, acting out and
enactment, should be preserved in the psychoanalytic literature.
While in acting out the analyst is kept (is able to keep himself) as a
(relatively conscious) *observing participant object*, in enactment the
analyst becomes an (always unconscious) *active participant object*.

The analyst's awareness of the enactment occurs *after* the action has been carried out.

If acting out is the black sheep in psychoanalytic treatment, dreams have been from the very beginning the darlings of psychoanalysts. When Freud asked his patients to speak freely, he discovered that they spontaneously began to tell him their dreams. His great insight was to realize that dreams were not merely a manifestation of mental activity during sleep, but that they were yet another aspect of the psychology of waking life. Freud could not believe his luck! More than thirty years later, he wrote: "Insight such as this falls to one's lot but once in a lifetime" (1932 [1931], p. XXXII). Dreams were interpreted by Freud as he had interpreted other aspects of waking life: memories, symptoms, or slips of the tongue. The interpretations of dreams became an essential feature of psychoanalytic treatments, although the way that dreams are used nowadays in clinical practice has greatly changed over the years, i.e. they no longer constitute the central task of the analysis. Furthermore, it is not impossible, although rare, that some analyses might even take place with no dreams being reported.

While the telling of a dream in analysis creates the possibility for the patient and the analyst to gain further understanding, acting out is the guardian of ignorance. Instead of assisting the analytic task, acting out attempts (not necessarily successfully) to dislodge the analyst from his analytic stance. Things get rather complicated when we consider that an action like the telling of the dream itself, independently of the content of the dream, can also be a form of acting out. This has been known to psychoanalysts for a long time and is well documented in the literature. A patient might tell a long dream to the analyst in such detail as to make interpretation of the content within the session impossible. Depending on the circumstances, it can be argued—let us say—that the patient is using the dream to "drown" the analyst, rather than as a means of communicating with him. What counts in this instance is the meaning of the action implied in the telling, rather than the meaning of the dream itself.

Dreams can be placed at the opposite extreme of acting out. In the context of an analytic treatment, we define dreams as the symbolic dramatic representations of past or present repressed wishes, traumas, and conflicts, which are told by the patient in the context of a session. In principle, dreams told by a patient in analysis can be considered more or less successful attempts by the patient to communicate to the analyst a situation of anxiety (Baranger, 1960).

For some patients the distinction between what is *symbolic* (like a dream, a slip of the tongue, etc.) and what is *action* has somehow become confused. At this point, let us say that the group of patients I have in mind might be closely linked to the thin- and thick-skinned narcissists, as described by Rosenfeld (1987). Rosenfeld saw the thick-skinned narcissist as someone who is insensitive to deeper feelings, whose envy is a major obstacle to the analysis. By contrast, the thin-skinned narcissist is hypersensitive and easily hurt; this type of patient seemed to have been made to feel persistently ashamed, vulnerable, and rejected.[1]

Herbert Rosenfeld defined narcissistic object relations as those in which a high degree of omnipotence in the subject contributes to an identification of himself with the object. I found his concept of *narcissistic omnipotent object relations* clinically very useful. What Rosenfeld had in mind was the way that disturbed patients use external objects as containers into which "they project those parts of themselves which are felt to be undesirable or which cause pain and anxiety ..." (1987, p. 20; see also Rosenfeld, 1964). The patient identifies so strongly with the object that he may feel he is the object, or that the object is himself. In Winnicott's terms, though one could say that the object "has become meaningful" for the patient, it remains nothing but a "bundle of projections" (Winnicott, 1969, p. 103).

Rosenfeld also advanced a theory of what he called *destructive narcissism*: the patient identifies with the destructive parts of the self, which are idealized and therefore experienced as attractive, making the patient feel omnipotent. One important aspect of this type of destructive narcissism is that, if the destructiveness is part of the patient's character structure, then "libidinal (that is, loving, caring, interdependent) object relationships ... are devalued, attacked, and destroyed *with pleasure*" (Rosenfeld, 1987, p. 22).

Rosenfeld's (and Winnicott's) patients were psychotic or seriously disturbed borderline people who, while giving the impression that they had no relationships, depended on the constant destruction of those relationships to maintain their narcissistic balance. The patients I would like to describe are not psychotic, nor are they patently borderline or openly perverted. They might be well "connected" to reality and appeared to have fairly "normal" relationships. Their destructive narcissism might only become truly evident in the psychoanalytic process.

One specific clinical aspect in the treatment of these patients is what Britton (1996) has described as their *difficulty*, which is of a particular kind: "(It) is the way that the analytic method itself is felt to be a threat (to the patient): its structure, its method, its boundaries". Despite their conscious wish to have analysis, and coming forward for treatment, these are patients who react very negatively to psychoanalysis itself. From the subjective experience of the analyst, the patient appears to have very little interest in being analysed. This could be described in Bion's terms: the activity of knowing, K, is inverted in these patients into an activity minus K (–K). They are compelled to prove themselves superior, and they frustrate any attempt at understanding on the part of the analyst. In fact, *misunderstanding the analyst's interpretations becomes central to the analytic process* (Bion, 1962). In some cases, the patient tries to seduce the analyst into a sadomasochistic game of scoring points. Either the analyst becomes the aggressor (and it does not take much for him to appear to become persecuting, since any interpretation offered by the analyst is experienced by the patient as an attack), or the analyst has to become the patient's victim and submit to the patient. The analysis itself becomes such a threat because the patient suffers from a *remarkable intolerance of psychic pain*, at times just hidden by a thin veil of arrogance. Unable to contain any psychic pain, he expels it into external objects through manipulation. He wants his objects to take on his agony, frustration, and anxiety, but he consequently feels persecuted by this very need. In the end, the need for an object (an *impossible* object, one which is supposed to help him get rid of his pain) provokes a range of intense aggressive fantasies, accompanied by fears of retaliation and vindictiveness. This process is partly motivated by intolerable envy, but envy cannot account for it.

On rare occasions, a short-lived flash of enlightenment breaks through, making the patient aware of just how ill he is. This is a fairly typical reaction encountered in the analysis: the patient falls into a state of depression, and compulsive suicidal thoughts appear in the sessions. Although these brief episodes never reach the intensity that would make the analyst concerned for the patient's safety, the suicidal thoughts have the eerie, convincing quality of being a "realistic" possible solution to the patient's problems; this quality is almost pathognomonic for these patients. In fact, the idea of suicide might appear as the only available alternative to their hidden fear of disintegration.

Therefore, it is understandable (though no less perplexing) that ignoring psychic pain might be for them preferable to insight, or feeling misunderstood preferable to being understood by the analyst. John Steiner (1993) has described similar clinical situations. He has made a distinction between *understanding* and *being understood*, sustaining that certain patients might not be interested in understanding themselves but might still have a need to be understood by the analyst. At the same time, he refers to the fact that, "A few patients appear to hate the whole idea of being understood and try to disavow it and get rid of all meaningful contact" (p. 132). Although Steiner adds that even this last group of patients needs the analyst to acknowledge and recognize their predicament, there seems to be a certain number of them for whom acknowledgement and recognition are impossible to accept. Ignorance and misunderstanding keep these patients alive; understanding is equated to disintegration and death.

In the context of these theoretical reflections, I would like to present a brief clinical vignette.

II

Mr N was born to a working-class family in an industrial town on the East Coast of the U.S.A. He was in his early forties, and was teaching European Literature at a university in the South of England. Among other things, he taught a course in psychoanalytic literary criticism. He had had a previous analysis in the States, which had lasted for about two years. Mr N grew up in a family environment which was always experienced by him as alien; he could never quite fit. His parents were fairly old by the time of his birth, and Mr N might have been an unwanted child. Father worked for many years at the same factory, had retired, and then died. Not much life to the image of this rather absent, weak father. The picture of his mother was predictably similar: a dedicated housewife, an undemonstrative mother, she appeared as a rather bland figure. Mr N never felt welcome in the family, nor had he felt comfortable in his relationships with his parents or with his siblings. He had three brothers and three sisters, the patient being the youngest. Mr N's account presented a picture of rigid, rather forced and non-spontaneous relationships within the family, greatly marked by a stifling religious atmosphere.

At the time of his first consultation, he had been married for about ten years to a rather shy, inhibited Canadian woman whom he had met while still in the States, through the activities of the Church. They had no children, and this was a source of great pain, frustration, and long-standing suffering. They had never discovered what was the cause of their infertility, but Mr N thought that he was responsible for it. Their attempts to conceive through different methods failed. Mr N felt enraged by all this, and spent a great deal of time at the beginning of his analysis complaining about it.

The analysis seemed to develop along fairly "normal" lines for a while. Typically, the patient developed an intense positive transference, with strong idealized features. This did not last long. During his third month of analysis, Mr N told me the following dream (his first):

He was undergoing certain kinds of tests. There were people around, among them the Head of Department of a rival University, who was sitting near by, watching. There was one particular man in a white coat, who took the patient's penis, put it between two screens, as if he were a doctor taking some kind of X-rays. "There is a bit of fluff", the guy said. There was another test, which consisted in some kind of rectal examination.

The patient called this a "homosexual dream", and seemed quite pleased with himself at having produced it. He identified himself as the patient under examination and said I was the doctor, looking for something wrong in his penis and in his potency. He thought the Head of Department represented a colleague of his, someone with whom he felt very competitive. Mr N thought that the "bit of fluff" was something soft in him, something feminine, that he did not want me to see. He said he felt exposed and vulnerable.

It was in fact true, and quite obvious to both of us, that the patient felt under examination: he felt I was judging him all the time, disapproving of who he was, and what he was doing. He felt he was performing all the time; he felt inadequate, invaded, and humiliated. Sometimes he was concerned about his sexual identity and wondered whether he was homosexual.

I acknowledged that he felt his potency was under examination in the analysis; I seemed to be examining who he was, what he was doing, and how was he performing. He felt excited at the idea of being rectally examined by me, and the presence of a competitor turned voyeur intensified the pleasure involved. Yet, I suggested, perhaps it was also I who was under close examination by him in the dream; he would have liked to examine my potency and my analytic capacities, so as to discover something soft, a "bit of fluff", instead of something strong and erect. He said that he was aware of measuring every word I said, and in his mind he gave me marks for my interpretations, feeling very triumphant when he thought I was "on the wrong track". So far, so good. This dialogue between a patient and an analyst could be seen as a fairly acceptable analytic exchange.

However, Mr N then said (with a tone of his voice that took me aback by its violence) that he sometimes wished, more than anything else, that I should feel as inadequate and vulnerable as he did. This was an intense conscious wish of his. He wanted to make me suffer in the same way that he thought I was making him suffer. He hated being a patient. He hated the analysis.

It soon became clear that interpretations, instead of producing relief or an opening for further psychic work, invariably provoked aggressive and envious reactions—which I was to see repeated on many future occasions. This was particularly the case in dreams and slips of the tongue. Ostensibly, Mr N wanted to please me—say, by telling me a dream. Nevertheless, after the initial honeymoon period, as soon as *any* interpretation was offered, he felt rejected and humiliated. This happened independently of whether the interpretation made sense to him. He desperately needed me to be a strong parental figure, but as soon as Mr N experienced me as such, he felt put down, denigrated, dismissed, and—on rare occasions—abandoned.

In the following session, Mr N claimed to feel misunderstood by everybody, and since he was absolutely convinced that nobody could ever understand his pain, he claimed that the analysis would never work. How could I possibly put myself in his shoes? What did I really know? Did I think that for all my analytic training I could understand him? This sequence was established as a pattern in the analysis. It is relevant to note that the interpretations of these manoeuvres were themselves transformed into a scenario in which he played the part of a suffering little boy tortured by an uncaring, heartless (father) analyst. Mr N had constructed an image of himself as a loving, generous person, who felt mistreated by others: there was no room in this picture for the way that he treated other people. He was convinced that I, as his analyst, only enjoyed making him feel belittled and impotent. In his mind, an analyst was merely an accessory in yet another perverse object relationship. As argued by Britton (1996), this propensity for malignant misunderstanding in and of, the transference is so characteristic of these patients that it makes suitability for analysis doubtful.

In a later session, he had the fantasy that he would cut his wrists and splash the blood all over my consulting-room, or alternatively, pull a gun and kill me. He insisted that I was not making enough efforts to understand him, and bitterly complained that I was ignoring his pain. He reported the following dream:

My father had died after having had a fight with me. I was alone in the room with him. Our family doctor came in and said: "Don't worry, I'll get you a birth certificate ..." (At this point, he paused, and then he said:) "Jesus! I said a 'birth certificate', instead of a 'death certificate'..."

Mr N remained silent for a while. In reality, he told me, he had a fight with his father the week prior to his father's death. The patient's mother had gone to New York City, to visit relatives, and it was then that the fight had taken place. They had made up by the time the father died, but the patient was afraid of having contributed to his death. "Real oedipal stuff", he commented. I thought that he too readily accepted this "oedipal stuff"; no other associations to the dream were forthcoming. I said that perhaps he had felt that there was not enough room for both of them, father and son, in the relationship; in fact, competition or rivalry had not been possible; it had been more a case of either his father, or him—the two of them could not exist together; father's death was his birth. Perhaps he wanted me to be like the family doctor, that I would certify his birth without any analysis of what was happening in the therapy. We had seen on previous occasions how the two of us could not exist together. Now, either he cut his wrists and killed himself, or he killed me; once again, there was no room for both of us.

Following this, he found himself "rehearsing" over the weekend how angry he was with me, and had become rather "obsessed" with these feelings. In the Monday session he shouted at me that he knew his marriage had been a "sick" (a word I had never used) relationship; he was aware of how dishonest he had been with his wife (for, among other things, he had a number of affairs during their marriage); yet—in spite of all the evidence—he still found himself blaming me for the failure of the marriage. He had wanted to separate from his wife for years, well before he came for analysis, and had given himself all sorts of pretexts for not doing so, but—as unreasonable as this was—he felt that I should have helped him to sort out the marriage. He claimed I had behaved "sadistically" in this respect towards him, although he could "almost" see that he could not justify this claim.

The patient reported on Tuesday that he had been thinking about Mary and Richard, a couple of friends and colleagues who were living in Rome. He had been planning to visit and stay with them the following autumn. He found out that Richard had been offered a grant to travel (by the university from which Mr N had originally graduated), and was going to be away around that time; Mr N was very excited at the thought of making love to Mary while Richard was away. Rome was such a romantic city! But why, he asked, would he want to have an affair with Mary? It did not make any sense to him. He went on to say that he had no respect for Richard, but got along very well with Mary. He had the thought: "Maybe I could do a better job than Richard". He was thinking about this while driving his car to the session, and found himself saying out loud: "I really love ... Richard!"—when he meant to say Mary. He felt puzzled, rather hopeless, and was very upset by this slip of the tongue.

There are many issues in this episode but I will only comment on one particular aspect. The fantasy about his friends and the corresponding unconscious slip regarding their names brought up intense anxiety in the patient. Mr N came face to face with his conflicts and dilemmas as regards his sexuality, the uncertainties concerning issues of sexual differentiation and homosexuality, and the question of otherness. I learnt then that Mr N did not think of himself just as a frustrated father: he wanted to be both mother *and* father, all in one. He confessed that he had conscious wishes of having breasts, so he could feed a baby; he pictured himself and the imaginary baby surviving very happily without a mother. Potentially, this was useful transference material; it presented a picture of how Mr N imagined and viewed the analytic relationship. Nevertheless, any suggestion I made in the form of an interpretation (whether connected to the transference, or not), was countered by an emphatic rejection from the patient.

The slip of the tongue (like on other occasions, dreams) was a source of information about Mr N's unconscious scenarios. How could it not be? Nevertheless, Mr N's internal world was divided between what gave him narcissistic satisfaction, and what deprived him of such satisfaction. His investment in work and relationships, and the whole of his value system, were aimed at underpinning and sustaining the grandiosity of his self. Mr N wanted above all to be admired so as to confirm that this grandiosity was real. He moved from intense idealization of his objects (the ones providing him with admiration) to devaluation of others (the depriving objects). While this gave him some temporary protection against his feelings of envy, Mr N was unable to develop a world of internalized object relationships that offered him enrichment and support, something he could build upon. The sheer experience of taking in an interpretation, the need to make space in his mind for the analyst as an internal object, would make him feel empty and a failure. In Winnicott's terms (1969), he felt he could not afford to place the object outside the area of his omnipotent control.

III

In Melanie Klein's view of the transference, the material offered by patients in a session not only revealed "the function of the ego", but also "the defences against the anxieties stirred up in the transference situation" (1952, p. 437). Klein further believed that the analytic reliving of past experiences led the patient to act out, turning away from the analyst "as he attempted to turn away from his primal object" (p. 437). Rosenfeld (1964) developed this further, suggesting that the intensity of the acting out (i.e. *partial*, or *excessive*) depended on the amount of hostility experienced by the subject in the original process of turning away from the primary object.

The patients I am discussing also have turned away from the primary object both prematurely and in hatred. But, in contrast to a large number of psychotic and borderline patients, there is no indication of past abuse or overt neglect in the patients' histories; this might explain why they are not as confused or as disturbed. The primary object was very likely physically present, and yet psychically absent and emotionally inadequate. The *premature turning away* from the primary object was accompanied by the creation of a self that was idealized as all loving and good, but which apparently did not need anybody or anything. Any dependency is later experienced as an act of humiliation perpetrated by the object; in the context of the analysis, any interpretation of the patient's needs represents an attack on the integrity of the self. Control and manipulation of the object become paramount, while at the same time the boundaries between self and others were kept blurred—more than blurred, they were *murky* in two senses: dark boundaries that are clouded and confused are also experienced as threatening and forbidding.

Although the patient had "managed" to turn away from the primary object, he does not achieve any separation from it. Separation from the primary object should promote, in normal circumstances, development and growth. As a consequence of the failure to separate, one relevant feature of the patient's character is the inability to mourn. There is no real mourning for the object, only intense and vicious feelings at the possibility of its loss, which is at the core of his incapacity for psychic pain. The absence of the object is not tolerated; the absent object has become the bad, persecuting, malicious object, never to be trusted, present only to make the subject suffer. Since absence only confirms the failure of the subject's omnipotent control over the world around him, it is exclusively experienced in terms of a pending catastrophe. In some cases, this catastrophe is averted by living in a manic *tempo*.

While the patient prematurely turned away from the object, the original experience of the primary object was that of the subject having *been ignored* by the object. Mutual ignorance is established between subject and object, which the subject survives at a price. The consequent premature turning away from the primary object takes place in hatred. (I prefer to speak in terms of hatred, rather than hostility, as suggested by Herbert Rosenfeld.) Ironically, it is this hatred that brings some life to the relationship. The fact that the subject is *able to hate* marks an important developmental achievement. At any rate, the patients are not just hostile or aggressive. The analyst is witness to a real hateful perversion of the goals of the analysis; the patient's main interest is to attack and destroy the analysis—and the analyst. The unconscious impulse is to dislodge the analyst from his analytic stance, confronting him with the need to *do* something, rather than merely interpret.

The capacity to hate is accompanied by the failure of love, which is always projected and seen in others. In analysis, the patient might feel that the only way of truly catching the analyst's attention is by *making the analyst hate him*; in provoking hate, a relative sense of self is achieved. From my own experience, and from the experience of people I have supervised, the patient succeeds in generating intense feelings of frustration and impotence in the analyst. The analyst begins to feel tyrannized by the patient's accusations, devaluation, and demands; sooner or later, hate in the counter-transference makes its appearance, which the analyst finds difficult to overcome. This is a real re-experiencing of the relationship with the primary object. A typical response on the side of the analyst is to be strongly tempted to attack the patient with interpretations, in a futile attempt to destroy the patient's grandiose self. It might be difficult for the analyst to disentangle himself from being identified with a disapproving judge who is busy condemning the patient for his actions. In these instances, the analyst makes interpretations from a superego position, which only confirms the patient's suspicion that the analyst is against him, that he hates him and, above all, that does not understand him. While in more or less normal and benign situations the interpretation of what patient and analyst might be enacting can push forward the analytic process, in these cases it only makes things worse.

The symbolic process that enables the subject to use his own dreams is pathologically affected. Dreams and other symbolic creations are produced in these analyses but cannot be used to generate insight. This represents a genuine *symbolic impoverishment* and greatly affects the creativity of those people who have achieved a moderate academic, professional, or artistic success. As a consequence of the patient's symbolic impoverishment, dreams, slips of the tongue, and any form of analytic narrative are not texts to be deciphered and interpreted: they are actions requiring a response, or the avoidance of a response. In fact:

> Words are used, not primarily to convey information, but as actions having an effect on the analyst, and the analyst's words are likewise felt as actions indicating something about the analyst's state of mind rather than offering insight into the patient. [Steiner, 1993, p. 131]

Dreams are used by the patient as instruments of intrigue, as a way to seduce or force the analyst to overlook something, or to divert his attention from something else happening in the session. Dreams, though symbolically created, become the equivalent of acting out: the patient uses his dreams to contain the projections of parts of himself, in the same way that he used his external objects. This is a similar process to Grinberg's *evacuatory dreams* (Grinberg *et al.*, 1967). Though Grinberg considered these as standing in an inverse relationship to acting out (i.e. the fewer dreams produced by the patient, the more acting out in the analysis, and *vice versa*), the main function of dreams for the patients I have in mind is to manipulate the analyst (rather than as a source of insight and working-through). The analyst's only alternative is to consider the dream exclusively from the point of view of the dreamer's experience (Pontalis, 1977). In other words, the question to be asked is not *what does this dream mean?* but *what is the patient doing with it to me*—and *why?*

IV

In a letter of November 15th, 1899, Freud writes to Heinrich Gomperz, a professor of Philosophy at the University of Vienna: "If you are willing to apply the philosopher's unrelenting love of truth also to your inner life, then I would be very pleased to play the role of the "other" in this venture ..." (Freud, 1961, p. 249). The analytic situation implies a partnership in which patient and analyst try to analyse the patient. The symbolically impoverished patients are unable to form this analytic partnership, and they establish a narcissistic partnership instead. This "other" that Freud had in mind is not allowed to exist.

Joyce McDougall (1986) has pointed out that the "narcissistic bliss in which separateness, sexuality and death are disavowed as external realities" is part of "everybody's psychic theatre". We are all compelled to "fill in the gap produced by the inconceivable existence of 'otherness'" (p. 51). We will each of us deal in our own individual ways with this separation, and with our need for narcissistic fulfilment. Some patients live within a psychic structure that does not give the "other" a separate place in their version of living. Real people in their lives have the function of occupying and filling up the holes that exist in the patients' psychic world. Their object relationships take place in a *narcissistic psychic space*, where self and objects can not be distinguished. The true existence of the object is a fiction for them, but they need real people to maintain the fiction. The patient *appears* to be dependent on his objects, but in fact they do not have a true, independent, psychic reality. The patient establishes a narcissistic relationship with himself through the objects that he selects to choose him. The real people who come to occupy the empty holes in the narcissistic space believe themselves to be real for the patient; they are, in fact, manipulated into being whatever the patient wishes. They are not just passive victims, but they risk not being aware of not existing as real objects for the patient. Needless to say, the analyst, whatever he interprets, feels frustrated.

While in *Mourning and Melancholia* Freud described a libidinal object (loved or hated) that continued to psychically exist after its death in the external world, and which needed to be mourned (1917 [1915]), the narcissistic object might not have existed (or been acknowledged as existing) in the first place, and thus cannot ever be lost or dead. The mourning process is necessarily affected. The primary object was ignored, and the subject has no intrapsychic space for it; the object only exists in an externalized world. It is an object that had no chance of having been introjected (as described by Melanie Klein), nor would it have constituted an "endopsychic structure" (as described by Fairbairn). The subject "cannot mourn the loss of the experiences he had never had" (Spillius, personal communication, 2000). This might account for the patient's feelings of emptiness and complaints of being eternally alone.

In the end, one could argue that, for these patients, the whole of the treatment becomes a form of acting out. What is resisted and rejected is not the specific meaning of a certain dream, a symptom, or a slip of the tongue, but the potential experience of change. They hate even their capacity to hate. Since he cannot develop "an internal sense of creating his own life" (Bollas, 1989, p. 34), the patient in analysis wants the treatment only to prove that he can do without it. The propensity for malignant misunderstanding and the incapacity for enduring psychic pain go hand in hand with the establishment of an omnipotent destructive self, which helps the patient to survive an always pending catastrophe. The omnipotent self has been assembled at the price of a true symbolic impoverishment.

Note

1. Anthony Bateman (1998, 1999) suggested that the two groups described by Rosenfeld move between thick-skinned and thin-skinned positions. Ronald Britton (1996) has expressed similar views, sustaining that inside every thick-skinned patient (there) is a thin-skinned patient trying not to get out, and *vice versa*.

References

Balint, E. (1954). Three faces of a transference neurosis. In: *Before I was I—Psychoanalysis and the Imagination*. London: Free Association Books, 1993.

Baranger, W. (1960). El sueño como medio de comunicación. In: W. & M. Baranger (Eds.), *Problemas del Campo Psicoanalítico*. Buenos Aires: Ediciones Kargieman, 1969.

Bateman, A. (1998). Thick- and thin-skinned organisations and enactment in borderline and narcissistic disorders. *International Journal of Psychoanalysis*, 79: 13–25.

Bateman, A. (1999). Narcissism in relation to violence and suicide. In: R. J. Perelberg (Ed.), *Psychoanalytic Understanding of Violence and Suicide*, New Library of Psychoanalysis no. 33. London: Routledge and The Institute of Psycho-Analysis.

Bion, W. R. (1962). *Learning from Experience*. London: Heinemann.

Bollas, C. (1989). *Forces of Destiny-Psychoanalysis and the Human Idiom.* London: Free Association Books.

Britton, R. (1996). Subjectivity, objectivity and the fear of chaos. *British Psycho-Analytical Society Bulletin, 32*(4).

Etchegoyen, H. (1986). *The Fundamentals of Psychoanalytic Technique.* London: Karnac.

Freud, E. L. (Ed.) (1961). *Letters of Sigmund Freud, 1973–1939.* London: The Hogarth Press, 1970.

Freud, S. (1917). *Mourning and Melancholia. S.E., 14.*

Freud, S. (1931). Preface to the third (revised) English edition. In: *The Interpretation of Dreams. S.E., 4.*

Grinberg, L. (1956). Sobre algunos problemas de técnica psicoanalítica determinados por la identificación y contraidentificación proyectivas. *Revista de Psicoanálisis, 13*: 507–511.

Grinberg, L. (1957). Perturbaciones en la interpretación por la contra-identificación proyectiva. *Revista de Psicoanálisis, 14*: 23–30.

Grinberg, L. (1963). Psicopatología de la identificación y contra-identificación proyectivas y de la Contratransferencia. *Revista de Psicoanálisis, 20*: 113–123.

Grinberg, L., Apter, A., Bellagamba, H. F., Berenstein, I., De Cereijido, F. et al. (1967). Función del soñar y clasificación clínica de los suenõs en el proceso analítico. *Revista de Psicoanálisis, 24*: 749–489.

Klein, M. (1952). The origins of transference. *International Journal of Psycho-Analysis, 33*: 433–438 [reprinted in *The Writings of Melanie Klein, Volume 3: Envy and Gratitude.* London: The Hogarth Press, 1975].

Limentani, A. (1966). A re-evaluation of acting out in relation to working through. *International Journal of Psycho-Analysis, 47*: 274–282 [also in *Between Freud and Klein—The Psychoanalytic Quest for Knowledge and Truth.* London: Free Association Books, 1989].

McDougall, J. (1978). *Plea for a Measure of Abnormality.* London: Free Association, 1990.

Pontalis, J.-B. (1977). *Entre le Rêve et la Douleur.* Paris: Gallimard.

Rosenfeld, H. A. (1964). On the psychopathology of narcissism: a clinical approach. In: *Psychotic States.* London: The Hogarth Press, 1965.

Rosenfeld, H. A. (1987). *Impasse and Interpretation—Therapeutic and Anti-therapeutic Factors in the Psychoanalytic Treatment of Psychotic, Borderline and Neurotic Patients.* London: Tavistock Publications.

Sandler, J. (1976). Counter-transference and role-responsiveness. *International Review of Psychoanalysis, 3*: 43–47.

Steiner, J. (1993). *Psychic Retreats—Pathological Organizations in Psychotic, Neurotic and Borderline Patients*. London & New York: Routledge.

Winnicott, D. W. (1969). The use of an object and relating through identifications. In: *Playing and Reality*. London: Penguin Books, 1974.

CHAPTER FIVE

Dreams of borderline patients

Peter Fonagy

R eflective function is the developmental acquisition that permits a child to understand another person's behaviour in mental state terms—feelings, attitudes, hopes, knowledge, imagination, pretense, intentions, and so on (Baron-Cohen, 1995; Baron-Cohen *et al.*, 1993; Morton & Frith, 1995). By attributing mental states to others, the child makes people's behaviour *meaningful* and predictable. This is crucially linked with the child's ability to label and find meaningful his own psychic experiences, an ability which arguably underlies the capacities for affect regulation, impulse control, and the experience of self-agency, the building blocks of the organization of the self.

What does the mind do with its experience, however, before the development of reflective or metacognitive function? My thesis, in this paper, is that dreams are residues of a primitive capacity to reflect upon mental states where thoughts, ideas, and feelings, the state of affairs of the mind at any one time, are represented in concrete images rather than as ideas *qua* ideas. I am suggesting that dreams are perhaps residues of a primitive infantile process of self-reflection which developmentally antedates full self awareness. The dream narrative is a depiction of the intrapsychic constellation which the primitive mind registers in the most adaptive way possible within its limited capacities.

This addition to a theory of dreaming is consistent with a number of major developments within dream theory, since Freud's extraordinary insights concerning the wish fulfilment function of dreams (Freud, 1900). I would like to draw your attention to three major developments in the clinical theory of dreaming:-

1. Many no longer consider dreams to be invariably wish fulfilments. They are as likely to be attempts at resolving conflict as expressions of it. Many recent contributors have stressed the adaptive function of dreams alongside the more traditionally accepted libidinal or aggressive function (Fosshage, 1983; Stolorow & Atwood, 1982).
2. It is now generally agreed that the act of dreaming is a significant act of re-presentation or symbolization. Numerous authors, beginning with Lewin, considered dreaming to be equivalent to the projection of an image upon a neutral surface (the dream screen) which the patient is at liberty to observe in much the same way as on waking he/she might watch a movie at the cinema or on television. Many have linked this notion to Winnicott's concept of transitional space (Winnicott, 1953).
3. It is now widely recognized that there is a critical transferential aspect to the interpretations of dreams in psychoanalysis. Dreams are not produced in isolation, but are rather dreamt "with the analyst in mind". As a consequence there are typical Jungian dreams, Freudian dreams, and Kleinian dreams, in just the same way as for Freud there were typical dreams about exams, falling, separation, escape, and finding oneself inadequately clothed in a public place. For example, I heard a Kleinian analyst report a patient's dream of eight soldiers marching side by side across a bridge. The speaker drew attention to the pun; eight abreast sounds like ate a breast.

Taking these developments together, I would like to suggest that some dreams are honest attempts on the part of the patient to adapt to the analytic situation where reflection is the paramount demand. As part of the "healthy" aspect of the transference, or what is traditionally called therapeutic alliance, the patient produces and then observes, their dream, where they depict as effectively as they are capable the state of affairs which they experience as currently pertaining in their mind. This, I believe, is true for all of us in analysis. There is, however, at this level a critical difference between patients who are capable of reflective function, by and large the traditional neurotic patient, and patients where this capacity is either partially or almost fully absent. With the neurotic patient, dreams quickly become an aspect of the unfolding narrative. When reflective capacity is available to the dreamer, we may anticipate that, even if the dream itself is rudimentary in terms of the extent of mentalization depicted, through secondary elaboration the dreamer will add meaning to the action of the protagonist and thus the dream sequence will in essence be impossible to differentiate from daytime fantasy mentation. In addition, dreams are consciously reacted to and those reactions are themselves reflected upon in the context of the analytic relationship. Thus, by the time the dream is reported to the analyst it very rarely bares any resemblance to the primitive infantile process of self-reflection, which in my view is at the core of all dreams.

The situation is very different for patients whose reflective capacity is compromised. Their dreams tend to be far closer to the primitive reflective root and do not benefit from mentalizing secondary elaboration. Patients with severe personality disorder have no reliable access to an accurate picture of their own mental experience, their representational world; they are unable to "take a step back", and respond flexibly and adaptively to the *symbolic, meaningful* qualities of other people's behaviour. Instead, they find themselves caught in fixed patterns of attribution, rigid stereotypes of response, non-symbolic, instrumental uses of affect—mental patterns that are not amenable to either reflection or modulation. They inhibit their capacity to think in terms of thoughts and feelings, prototypically as an adaptation to experiences of severe and chronic maltreatment. The vulnerable child, confronted with a care-giver who harbours frankly malevolent feelings and ideas towards him, may have little option but to inhibit or disavow thinking in terms of mental states altogether.

A number of authors have noted that important qualitative differences mark the dreams of borderline patients. The frequent depiction of non-human non-intentional objects, the portrayal of animals (e.g. reptiles or invertebrates such as worms etc.) to whom we all might have difficulty in attributing mental states, the very bizarreness of their dreams, all point to the absence of mentalizing elaboration as a consequence of partial failure of symbolization. Nevertheless, these dreams should be regarded as reflections, albeit of a primitive kind. The patient attempts to depict their experience of their thoughts and feelings, even if they are unable to enrich, elaboratively, this reflection. In fact, in the absence of genuine reflection as part of the analytic discourse, clinically dreams might be the only way the analyst might gain access to the inner world of the patient. In my view for borderline patients, although not for neurotic cases, Freud's "royal road" remains an apt metaphor (Freud, 1900).

The alien part of the self—the introject of the inaccurately mirroring other which is experienced as part of the self—often achieves representation in the dreams of borderline patients. Most often the image is one of penetration of the body (or physical self) by a parasitic being. Dream narratives can seem like stories by Roald Dahl. Technological advances have not left this aspect of life untouched either. A severe borderline and violent patient of mine dreamt that:

> his computer was taken over by a virus which "ate" its way into his programs.

The same man dreamt that:

> he was standing inside a drum which he should have been able to control by moving in specific directions except that the drum in his dream "seemed to have a will of its own" and where the drum went he had to go.

The fragile and vulnerable true self was encased in a larger and more powerful false structure which controlled him—an apt description of the state of affairs pertaining in his mind.

In clinical work with such patients the approach I am proposing has several critical implications. First, and most important, the patient, in providing the analyst with their dream, is not conveying an unacceptable repudiated impulse. If only they had the mental wherewithal to repudiate impulses, repress them and re-present them in disguised form, their pathology would be of far less severity. Thus, interpreting the impulse *per se* on the basis of the dream will be unlikely to lessen or reduce the patient's anxiety. An impulse may be depicted in the dream, but the critical contribution by the patient is the mere depiction of the impulse, not the work involved in creating disguise in order to avoid censorship.

A second and related point, is that the patient's report of the dream is fairly close to being their best attempt at self-reflection. If their reflective capacity is disabled by conflict, usually rooted in severe multiple trauma, all that may be accessible to them is this infantile reflective capacity. This is what I mean by the dream being an "honest attempt at reflection". It is part of the patient's attempt at collaborating with their understanding of the analytic goal and should always be interpreted as such.

A third and somewhat contentious issue, is that the dreams of such patients often exist principally at the "manifest level". With neurotic patients we are forced to "dig deep", to "find the true meaning" behind the patient's visual imagery. With borderline patients the elements of the dream are frequently far closer to the surface and far simpler in structure, depicting aspects of the patient's mind (thoughts, feelings, ideas) in ways which, for neurotic individuals, would not require dream interpretation to gain access to. In fact, they could, and do, achieve it automatically and very likely without analytic help.

Fourthly, as a consequence of the absence of secondary elaboration, the patient's dreams tend to be closer to their subjective experience and carry intense emotional valence. Borderline patients are far more likely to experience both intense pleasure and intense anxiety associated with the experience of dreaming. This is readily understandable in view of the primitive nature of the reflective process which re-emerges as part of night-time mentation.

Fifth, an independent reason for the intensity of patient experience of their dreams comes from the dysfunctional psychic reality which characterizes the mental functioning of individuals with severe personality disorder. The dominance of an early form of experience in psychic life, psychic equivalence, results in the dream ideas feeling as if they were actually experience. The young child equates mental contents with physical reality. What is out there must be in the mind, and what is in the mind must be out there. The mental world is not yet seen as representational, the "as if" aspect is still missing. Thus, for the borderline patient, dreams often are reality simply by virtue of the fact that it was thought about. They are more likely to conceive of dreams as foretelling the future or simply depicting present daily realities. The very act of interpretation may be anathema for such patients—the dream is what it is; it is inconceivable that it should stand for something else.

The example of Mr S

The first case is Mr S, a violent twenty-seven-year-old individual who was discharged from his six-year therapy with a woman psychotherapist because of his abusive and threatening behaviour. He was an individual prone to rage, largely associated with alcohol abuse. He reported transient psychotic-like episodes marked by visual illusions, experienced intense anxiety as well as profound depression. He frequently shouted and screamed at me and I felt frightened and frustrated as well as bewildered in his presence. He had been severely maltreated as a child by a brutal, drunken father. He had scars on his back, evidence of early abuse.

He had a profound fear of communication. As a child he had difficulty learning to write, fearing that he would betray himself in his writing and he deliberately distorted his handwriting to be able to fill the maximum amount of space with the minimum number of words. His associations similarly lacked depth, resonance, and evocativeness. The content of his utterances repeatedly left me with a sense of emptiness which I gradually recognized was something that he experienced.

Two months into his analysis he brought his first dream. He started the session describing in painful detail his journey from the underground station including commenting on the houses, the railings, the cracks in the pavement. I noted that he made no mention of the people he must have encountered. I said: "I think you would like me to know how hard it is for you to come and see me". He replied that no effort was involved but that he was tired because he had had a bad dream.

The dream was of a bureau with many drawers. He spent a long time finding the key. He knew that the drawers should be full but when he opened each in turn they were empty.

Explaining the dream, he mentioned that at work he kept his ideas locked away in a filing cabinet, not in the desk drawers where they would be more accessible. He was silent for a while then started talking about aspects of the building we were in which impressed him: its size, its grandeur, its many rooms. I said: "I think you are very frightened of having to look for your ideas and feelings in here because you feel that you will only find emptiness in yourself and in me". He replied that there were so many people trying to get out of the station that evening that he was frightened that he might never get to his session. This encouraged me to say that he also seemed frightened of closeness to me because it might replace his emptiness in a way that might make him feel confused, suffocated and trapped. He did not respond. I felt that he truly did not understand what I had in mind.

This was an episode from early in his analysis and also, autobiographically speaking, early in my work with violent borderline patients. Reading my notes on the case, I am in some ways impressed, but in some ways disappointed with my handling of Mr S's first dream. Conceiving of his dream as a rudimentary attempt at reflection, makes it clearer that Mr S was depicting his desperation about the emptiness which he experienced as his mind. He felt the drawers should have been full; he felt pressure from me to bring ideas, depicted in the pressure of people emerging from the station, but was unable to retrieve them, to pull them out from his mind. He was missing the key to understanding. He was impressed with all the ideas I was putting to him but he was impressed merely by their number or their appearance, not by their content. My statements felt empty to him. I was referring to feelings and thoughts which were empty containers that had long lost their contents. He was aware that it was him who had locked the ideas away, but was far more acutely aware of my incompetence in finding them. The dream might have been more accessible if I had communicated my understanding of his frustration at my failure to provide more than empty words, more than boundaries (cracks and railings). He was longing for relief from his experience of emptiness which in his mind could only be achieved through my offer of real assistance.

Let me elaborate on these points with a second dream, this time towards the end of the first year of the analysis. The dream was triggered by my lateness in arriving for one of his sessions. His reaction was extraordinary rage. He swore at me at the top of his voice, accused me of unprofessional conduct, of sabotaging his treatment and being totally unable to assist him. He questioned my sanity and accused me of being dishonest. He brought a dream to the next session.

He was in an art gallery. He thought in a vague way that I was there too. The striking thing to him about the dream was that people that he knew were hanging as photographic exhibits.

His association was to something he had seen on children's television: a speaking cartoon drawing on the wall that was apparently frustrated because its position was fixed. I said that perhaps the dream was telling us that his mental pictures of me and others were like photographs, not capable of reacting. I said that I thought that this actually distressed him but it could not be any other way because he was terrified when I acted in ways that he did not expect. He was able to respond to the interpretation and talk briefly about feeling frightened the previous day that I had been involved in a car accident and that I might be dead.

The dream was helpful in showing me the barrenness of his representation of people, their two-dimensional and unchangeable character. On reflection, the striking thing about the dream is his vague experience of me as a person beyond a photographic exhibit: there but not there, not yet clearly depicted but so intensely needed. His need, of course, was not for an affectional bond, however entangled or ambivalent, that one might expect of a neurotic patient. The need was for someone else to look at the pictures with him, to help him experience who they were as people, rather than simply to see them as photographs. With hindsight, I should have drawn his attention to the budding and shadowy awareness of me as a real other and how his terror of my unpredictability was easier to understand if we thought about just how fragile this vague sense of my presence was for him during the sessions, even when my physical presence was guaranteed. The inchoate image of me was such a marked contrast to the other representations of people, securely bounded by frames, solidly screwed into the gallery walls.

A final dream from this analysis might help illustrate the

progress that it is possible to achieve even with someone as severely incapacitated as Mr S. For two years I worked hard with Mr S, not at uncovering deep-seated conflicts, not at providing subtle insights, but more simply at recognizing his mental chaos, exploring triggers for feelings, identifying small changes in his mental states, highlighting our differences in perceptions of the same events, bringing awareness to the intricacies of the relationship between action and meaning, and placing affect into a causal chain of concurrent mental experience. In general I adopted a non-pragmatic, elaborative, mentalistic stance which placed a demand on Mr S to focus on my mental state as it struggled to reflect and understand the oftentimes dramatic shifts and swings of his perceptions and emotions.

In this process, he did "rediscover" the traumatic impact of his mother's attempted suicide, as well as the devastating impact of his father's physical abuse.

In one session he talked of his parents peering at him from the past, which he linked to an image of two sets of red eyes staring at him from the darkness like dogs. At the end of that session I had to ask him to make a couple of small changes in the times of his sessions two weeks hence.

Although he had appeared agreeable to these, in the next session he refused to lie down on the couch. His discontent quickly emerged as he complained about people who lived in denial, preferring not to know. By contrast he was someone incapable of living in bad faith. People just looked away and lived a lie. He told me about building a bed for a friend who was coming to stay in a couple of weeks' time. I said: "It seems that you no longer know how far you can have faith in me. At the moment it feels safer to construct your own couch rather than rely on my support".

After a brief silence he recalled two dream fragments.

One was about a lion which, to his surprise, he kept at home. The other, more disturbing, was about a man who was apparently being executed by someone who took two small red balls out of his pocket, as if he was going to give change to someone, and hammered them into the other's head. He was unable to look but none the less knew that this would kill the man.

The executioner reminded him of his father and the lion of a toy he had had as a child and which he had subjected to "terrible abuse".

He remembered that its mane had completely disappeared. I said that he wished me to know that the changes that I called small felt devastating to him and that if I, as the lion, was to suffer terrible abuse then I would learn how he felt and this would help him cope with his sense of not mattering. He acknowledged what I said, but continued to stare at the foot of the couch.

I sensed his shame and his anger. Eventually he volunteered that the lion had been a present from his father and that its eyes had been red but were missing in the dream. Referring to the red eyes of the previous session, I wondered if he felt one or other of us might be killed if we were forced to see things from the other's standpoint. He looked at me for the first time in the session and I noticed that he was crying. Through his tears he recounted that his father, having been away, saw that the lion he had given his son was dirty and damaged and severely beat the six-year-old Mr S. He remembered his father screaming at him: "I'll beat some sense into your head. Now you can see how it feels". I said: "I think you are terrified of me hammering my crazy ideas into you. If you try to see things from my point of view you would be driven crazy". He suddenly got up and lay down on the couch. There was silence, but also a mutual experience of communication. Eventually he said that he could not imagine that coming to analysis could ever make him feel happy, but he did feel that he had more space.

Mr S had a long analysis, lasting over nine years. During this time it emerged that he had been sexually abused, anally penetrated, by his father, as had his sister and they were able to confirm each other's memories. Mr S is now married with a child and comes to see me now and again a dozen years after his treatment began. It is important to know that he is a loving father and there is no hint of any kind of trans-generational transmission of maltreatment.

What is most moving in my recent contacts with him is his continued but consistent struggle in trying to understand what is happening in his mind; why he is feeling sad or angry, anxious or guilty. Interestingly, he often uses his dreams to assist him in understanding himself. He does not look for hidden ideas in the dreams, just for clues about how things that have happened to him have impacted on his feelings and thoughts. I think he has much to teach clinicians working with dreams of borderline patients.

The dreams of Miss R

Miss R was an attractive twenty-two-year-old doctoral student, the eldest of four daughters, all within four years of age, the middle two being twins two years younger than herself. Her father was a wealthy film producer, her mother a barrister who was working during much of her early childhood. She was left in the care of a nanny and a housekeeper from three weeks of age. She sought solace from the neglect in endless imaginative play. She had a dolls house theatre from early childhood to pre-adolescence in which she compulsively produced plays.

She appeared rapidly to engage in the analysis, exalted its value, wept and laughed, thoughtfully reflected and manifested anger, accepted and contributed to interpretative work, and yet I had a powerful impression that her experience of herself was not genuine. She would speak about the remarkable progress that we were making, or how "good" a particular session was, but in the counter-transference, I felt an emptiness or shallowness after such remarks. I wondered what it was that needed to be kept at a safe distance by such idealization. I felt I did not know her as a person; gradually I understood that everything was contradicted by everything else. I would get momentary images of her which would obliterate previous ones, only in their turn to be obliterated by a more recent episode. She would present herself as sentimental and sensitive, but this would be belied by a later session where she would show callousness verging on cruelty. At times she could appear depressed, hopeless, and self-hating, at other times, triumphant and grandiose. Unlike neurotic ambivalence, there was no sense of continuity between these different personae.

Gradually, I understood that the pictures she painted were not genuine self-perceptions, but rather they were projected in order to manipulate my feelings towards her. Her apparent callousness and arrogance was not a reflection of malevolence. Rather, she was demanding that I should enact a relationship with a malevolent person: be forgiving or critical, frightened or angry or whatever was needed. It slowly dawned on me that there was no relationship between her representations of herself within the analysis and what she actually felt. It was not even that she was a hysteric playing a series of roles, because such patients reveal a common inner core which is protected by the dissimulation. Her alternating and unpredictable self-representations *actually* constituted her subjective experience of her existence; there appeared to be no core on which she could draw. In Winnicott's sense, there was no true self.

In the transference, it was difficult for Miss R to conceive of me as a separate object. I quickly became essential to her life, "as the air she breathed", as she would put it. I was but a part of her, someone with exactly her interests and priorities. She sometimes seemed to assume that I had read everything that she had read, that I knew everyone that she knew, and that I liked the same paintings and photographs that she appreciated. She showed surprisingly little curiosity about my family or circumstances, almost as if what she already knew was all that there was to know. She made constant and outrageous demands for my attention, and assumed that besides her I had little to concern me.

Separateness became impossibly painful; she sometimes phoned me several times a day no matter where I was. Increasingly I had the feeling that she had to get in touch whenever she felt lost within herself; I carried her identity, and therefore had to be kept under total control. She would phone me late at night to seek my opinion about trivial practical dilemmas, but at the root of all her calls was a very real feeling that by herself she could not locate herself. Of course at such times suicidal ideas were quick to emerge and even though the threats were momentary and clearly manipulative, they were frightening and real.

Miss R had a dream in which she depicted herself as made out of chicken wire, a kind of wire mesh image. Her associations were to the famous experiment by Harlow, on monkeys fed by a wire mesh rather than a cloth "mother".

I thought her depiction was genuine, accompanied by real sadness and a sense of loss. It would be inaccurate to think of this as an indication of the early roots of her difficulties. The dream depicts Miss R's infantile, confused, and bewildered core or true self, clinging desperately to an empty, wire mesh shell of a self-representation, where she senses no substance, no protection, and no fulfilment of a desire for identity.

While this was a helpful and productive image, it was also a rare episode. Much of my time with Miss R was spent as a helpless and oftentimes clueless victim of her manipulativeness and control. She danced around the consulting room, put her feet up on the wall, rolled off the couch, constantly turned round to look at me, made phone calls during sessions on her mobile phone, sat outside the consulting room door while waiting for me to finish with my previous patient, missed sessions with feeble excuses, but then rang me late at night to check that I was still around, and so on. A basic technical problem was to deal with these enactments, trying to identify their immediate cause. She needed to make me into something which I had to briefly become and identify with, at the same time as locating the anxiety that propelled her to externalize an alien part of herself into me. But while I became another I could not think about her.

In one session, about eight months into her analysis, she came into the room clearly agitated. She paced up and down without saying a word. Then she started speaking, expressing the hope that she was my sole patient. She felt psychoanalysis would work much better if, for each patient, there was a specially designated analyst. She went on to recall an experience from her unsuccessful relationship with an older man. They were having sex, and her excitement reached such a pitch that she felt totally lost in the experience. She recalled feeling terrified that she was capable of being "swallowed up" by such excitement. I indicated that she wished for a unique relationship with me, so that she could swallow me up in her excitement, and I would lose my threatening identity as an analyst. She recalled that in her lovemaking she dealt with her sense of losing her identity by scratching her lover's back very hard with her fingernails, so powerfully that he cried out in pain and lost his erection. I thought that the interaction revealed just how essential it was for Miss R to externalize the threat she experienced by creating anxiety in her partner, who in this way became her terror as I did in the transference. I said, "You want to be my only patient because it is terrifying for you to think that your control over me is not absolute. You feel confused when you think about me in any way other than being with you. I think you need me to feel involved and excited by thinking of your sexual life, because then you can truly feel that I am under your control, and you feel that you know where I am and what I am thinking". She responded by telling me about a terrifying dream she had had the previous night.

She had dreamt about wild horses which were threatening to overrun and destroy a rickety and messy stables. She was inside the stables, and was terrified of being trampled, but a tall man stepped in front of her and magically quietened the horses.

From the way she told the dream, particularly in the way she took pride in the person's capacity to quieten the horses, it was clear that the dream was not a wish-fulfilment dream about the transference, although that was her conscious association. The man was described as having a unique capacity to communicate with animals, a capacity which on previous occasions *she* had claimed to possess. I saw the dream differently from her. She was the tall man and the wild horses depicted her internal object representation, over which, in reality, she had only very tenuous control. I said that she wished she were the man in the dream, who could control the feelings and ideas which constantly threatened to destroy the rickety stables of her mind. I empathized about how hard it must feel to experience her feelings as totally out of control, and therefore always dangerous. I said that I understood that it was paradoxically easier to make people outside wild, like the horses in her dream, because they still felt more accessible to her control than the messy stables of her internal world. She responded that she often wished that people did not take her so seriously. Why couldn't people play, as she used to do as a child? She talked about her dolls' house dramas, and the tragedies she could enact using animal figures. She started on an intellectual trail, to talk of the role of tragedy as a portrayal of all basic human conflicts. I interrupted, and said "I think you would prefer me not to know how vital this way you have found of dealing with me is to you. I think you feel in great danger unless you feel you are in control of what I think and feel". As we talked gradually her agitation receded and she was able to lie down and talk.

As in this session, over the course of two years, the impasse in our work was slowly resolved, and Miss R's analysis became more productive. There was no turning point, no dramatic insight linked to this change. My resolution and almost dogged persistence is the only plausible account of the improvement. New ways of using mental representations started to emerge.

For example, she had a dream in which she was hiding in the flat of a man, K, whom she was attracted to, but had rejected. She knew that K had found another girlfriend.

The previous day's session she was overcome by sadness, realizing, after a period of manic denial when she tried to persuade me that K did not matter to her, how she seemed to need to destroy any possibility of a good relationship.

In the dream K was bringing his girlfriend back for the night. He found Miss R already in his bed; she did not see the girlfriend but felt petrified, aware of a terrible humiliation, but thankfully then the dream ended. In associating to the dream she revealed that she thought that she had called a warning out to K from the bed. I noted that a qualitatively different state of reflectiveness was perhaps present in the dream. I said, "I think what makes all this a lot harder to talk about is that a part of you secretly feels quite convinced that when K saw you in his bed, he would say that he realized what a mistake he had made and he would send his girlfriend away and welcome you back. I think you know that this is a dream and you feel terribly humiliated when the dream ends". I added that I thought yesterday and at other times a similar sort of thing happened between us—that she initially hoped I would go along with her dream of secret triumph, but yesterday we had got closer to the reality of the actual her.

Miss R did get "better"; in the third year of her analysis she started a relationship and her depressions ameliorated even earlier. But her progress was limited. No longer troubled by feelings of emptiness, she left the analysis and moved countries again. I hear from her regularly and it is clear that she was not "cured" by her analytic experience.

With these three dreams, I hope to have illustrated a change in the quality of representation that can take place in the dreams of borderline patients within an analysis. To start with, Miss R simply depicted the state of affairs that the analysis found her in. Her true self, the terrified infant monkey, clung desperately to an empty container, the wire mesh mother. The image depicts the same appreciation of lack of substance that Mr S's empty drawers depicted.

Her dream of wild horses gave a much clearer perspective on her state of mind. She showed some awareness of the impulses and feelings which she could not yet name, but could represent their existence as well as the threat they posed for the stability of her internal world. The psychic equivalence mode which characterized this experience lent it the feeling of danger and destruction which she found inescapable. As adults we know that mere feelings cannot really destroy our sense of identity, that ideas are not really a threat to our continued existence. To the small child, the infant in all of us, this is by no means so clearly evident. If the psychic equivalence mode of functioning dominates, as it clearly did for Miss R, the only alternative to experiencing feelings might be to create them externally, usually in other people. While this is helpful from the point of view of our internal economy, it is evidently unhelpful in terms of social adaptation, in making friends and influencing people. You will not be surprised to hear that Miss R was a very lonely person.

In the third dream from Miss R's analysis, there was strong evidence of a capacity to distinguish internal and external reality. In fact her dream turned on the dawning recognition that the mere fact of creating an idea does not make it true. In her childhood, she was obsessed by her dolls' house dramas where it seemed that she enacted many of the feelings that were inaccessible to her through her natural process of reflection. At these times, her psychic reality was in a pretend mode, completely isolated from what felt real and actual. Sadly, through much of her analysis, she was able to maintain this form of existence and pretend with ideas, talk, hypothesize and interpret, yet experience too little of what was real for genuine connections to be made. Had she stayed in analysis for longer this might have been more adequately addressed. As it is, I believe she remains a sad woman, struggling to contain and control unmetabolized and unlabelled feelings and thoughts.

Conclusion

Dreams are important, not just because they help us understand what is happening in our patients' minds. Any part of the patient's material, free association, non-verbal gestures, dramatic enactment, might lead us to this end. More importantly, dreams give us a window on the patient's current capacity to understand their own psychological state of being—where they are, and how far they have got on the road to recovering reflective function.

Using dreams in this way, we must be careful that we do not obscure the patient's struggle by compensating for a lack of reflection, giving meaning to material which, as yet, has little substance. Perhaps we find ourselves doing this because we are horrified by the self-inflicted destruction of mentalization in our patients. When we see physical disfigurement we often look away. I believe that when we see its psychological equivalent, our counter-transference is no less dangerous. We have to try hard not to preconsciously ignore our patients' struggles, make false assumptions concerning their reflective capacity and, in the case of dreams, over-interpret them. If we do this, if we see more in the patients' material than there is, we are merely performing the mental elaboration which they failed to do and converting the patient's experience from a physical into a psychic one.

It is at this point that I believe that many psychotherapists "lose" their patients to meaningless and sometimes endless dialogue which one of my child patients termed "psychotherapese". As analysts we often encounter, in supervision and elsewhere, therapeutic processes which have reached an impasse where patient and therapist both speak but nobody listens. Fixed and rigid patterns of interaction are repeatedly enacted without reflection. I think this is the commonest reason for the failure of psychotherapeutic treatment with border-line patients. Dreams, as all effective components of treatment, are at once potential culprits and possible panacea. I hope this paper has helped to distinguish between the two.

References

Baron-Cohen, S. (1995). *Mindblindness: An Essay on Autism and Theory of Mind*. Cambridge, MA: Bradford, MIT Press.

Baron-Cohen, S., Tager-Flusberg, H., & Cohen, D. J. (1993). *Understanding Other Minds: Perspectives from Autism*. Oxford: Oxford University Press.

Fosshage, J. (1983). The psychological functions of dreams: a revised psychoanalytic perspective. *Psychoanalysis and Contemporary Thought*, 6: 641–669.

Freud, S. (1900). The interpretation of dreams. *S.E.*, 4 and 5: 1–715.

Morton, J., & Frith, U. (1995). Causal modeling: a structural approach to developmental psychology. In: D. Cicchetti & D. J. Cohen (Eds.), *Developmental Psychopathology, Volume. 1: Theory and Methods* (pp. 357–390). New York: John Wiley.

Stolorow, R., & Atwood, G. (1982). The psychoanalytic phenomenology of the dream. *Annual of Psychoanalysis, 10*: 205–220.

Winnicott, D. W. (1953). Transitional objects and transitional phenomena. *International Journal of Psycho-Analysis, 34*: 1–9.

CHAPTER SIX

The "oracle" in dreams:
the past and the future in the present

Rosine Jozef Perelberg

I n this paper, I suggest that in the early stages of many analyses some patients' dreams are predictive of the future course of the analysis. These dreams contain a condensed narrative about the transference relationship and encapsulate a narrative that will unfold as the analysis progresses. Although the analyst may be aware of the crucial relevance of such dreams at the time they occur, it is only retrospectively, at a later stage in the analysis, that these dreams may be more fully comprehended. Moreover, there is a specific experience that is conveyed in the account of these dreams, that is felt by the analyst in the counter-transference, but only slowly understood as the analysis unfolds. The analytic task is to change the course anticipated by these dreams, and introduce a difference in the "prediction" these dreams make.

Although the psychoanalytic literature contains some references to the first dream in a patient's analysis (e.g. Stekel, 1943; Greenacre, 1975; Beratis, 1984), there is a scarcity of papers on the subject. Stekel (1961) has suggested that first dreams in analysis may express the dreamer's whole story, and are mainly derived from real-life traumatic experiences. Bessleer also linked the first dream in analysis to early childhood memories and suggested that first analytic dreams may indicate that the patient experiences entering analysis as a return to the maternal breast. Franco and Levine (1969) constructed psychological profiles of the dreamer on the basis of such first dreams. Beratis (1984) has recently discussed the relevance of first dreams in analysis, although she seems to interpret this first dream directly from its manifest content, without waiting for the patients' associations or relating them to the transference situation. None of these papers relate first dreams to the transference situation and the course of the analytic process itself.

If *The Interpretation of Dreams* (Freud, 1900) marks the inauguration of psychoanalysis and the discovery of the unconscious, many elaborations, such as that of infantile sexuality, repression, phantasy, transference, the Oedipus complex, and castration were still to be developed by Freud. More specifically relevant to the understanding of the thesis of this paper is the notion of repetition compulsion. In his 1920 paper, Freud pointed to the existence of "traumatic dreams", which are "endeavouring to master the stimulus retrospectively, by developing the anxiety whose omission was the cause of the traumatic neurosis" (1920, p. 320). If the present contains a repetition of the past, this past constitutes, in the Sandlers' terminology, a template for the future (Sandler & Sandler, 1994) upon which it is the analytic task to intervene.

From 1920 onwards, Freud confronted the limits of psycho-analytic understanding (Freud, 1920, 1924, 1937). If the topographical model of the mind suggested an intrinsic link between drives and their representations (ideas at the core of *The Interpretation of Dreams*), the structural model of the mind and the concept of the death drive postulated a drive that did not correspond to a representation, but expressed itself through repetition compulsion. The topographical model of the mind emphasized a psychic world *full of representations*, whereas the structural model of the mind pointed out the *radical heterogeneity of psychic life* (Green, 1998, p. 83). Freud became progressively more interested in understanding phenomena which are potentially at the limits of symbolic representation, not only due to mechanisms of repression, splitting, denial, and negation, but also because they relate at the same time to something profoundly destructive in the psychic sphere that breaks through the capacity of the mind to contain it. These ideas are specifically relevant to a modern conceptualization of dreams, and *the understanding that many patients act rather than remember*. Dreams themselves may be viewed not only through what they symbolize, but also in terms of what may be understood as their function. This thesis expands the understanding of dreams from meaning to the experience they induce both in the dreamer and in the analyst to whom the dream is related.

My thesis about the "predictive" relevance of dreams in analysis subsumes a number of modern ideas about dreams and their interpretation:

- Firstly, the idea that dreams are expressions of patients' current states of mind.
- Secondly, there is a connection between dreams, the transference and the analytic process.
- Thirdly, it is not only the content of dreams that is addressed in an analysis, but also the *experience* brought by dreams to both the patient and the analyst (Pontalis, 1974). It is the detailed understanding of these experiences in any analysis that will lead to meaningful insight (Sedlak, in this volume).
- Fourthly, and as a consequence of the above, my thesis takes into account theories that suggest a shift in the quality and usage of dreams by the patient during the course of an analysis (Khan, 1972; Stewart, 1973; Pontalis, 1974; Segal, 1986; Quinodoz, 1998).

I will now discuss some of the clinical material that led me to my formulations.

Maria and the block of cement

My experience of Maria at the first consultation was bizarre. I could not understand it and the description that occurred to me was that "a part of her is not there". It was not that she seemed distracted, but that there was a sense of absence that impinged on me with a hypnotic quality. I experienced a deep heaviness, that led me to feel as if I was going to fall asleep. I decided to pursue the idea that "a part of her was not there", in an attempt to verify her experience of herself. Maria immediately seemed to understand what I was talking about and said that she felt that, since her relationship with Alex, a boyfriend some thirty-years earlier, she had disconnected herself, a part of her never "being there" again. This response, that allowed me to think that she could connect with my experience of her, helped me to decide to accept her for treatment.

In the following weeks, this hypnotic quality was pervasive in the consulting room. I was left feeling uncomfortable about barely managing to remain awake during Maria's sessions, even if I had felt alert just before she arrived.

A month into treatment Maria had the following dream:

There were three women and a huge block of concrete suddenly fell on top of them. The women were completely flattened and then started to rush about crazily. Maria said it looked like a cartoon.

She said it was a dream, but it did not feel like a dream. In this session we talked about her experience that this had not felt like a dream because it was so integral to the way she felt—that she had lost her feelings and her three-dimensionality and had become flattened. It also concerned her experience of feeling disconnected from herself in the present, and her way of relating to me, of flattening me in the sessions. I could then also understand the experience of having concrete inside my head, of feeling unable to think in her presence.

The dream which "had not felt like a dream" took on another layer of meaning, expressing a terror that she was going to be "hit" by the analysis and would not be able to cope. Retrospectively this was also a prognostic dream, a description of what was going to happen both to her and to the analytic process.

During the first year of analysis some important themes emerged, which we worked on very slowly over subsequent years. We had access to these themes primarily via dreams which functioned as markers of what was happening for Maria in the analysis: her rage towards her mother whom she experienced as inaccessible to her, and as "not being there" either, her phantasy of violence in sexual intercourse, her perceptions of her physical body (which included both her fear and rejection of her femininity and of the babies she might have been able to produce) and, ultimately, overriding all these previous themes, her belief that it was dangerous to experience any feelings (either positive or negative) towards me.

In spite of a great deal of material slowly surfacing, I continued to feel that "a part of her was not there". For instance, she would not consciously remember things from one session to the next. Some years later she was to refer to her memory of how, in that first year, her heavy eyes just wanted to close.

She let me know, at the end of that first year, that she was feeling more alive. She had started to buy newspapers, something she had never done before in her life, and was also starting to do jobs in her house, which she had completely neglected for years.

Four weeks after the end of the first summer break Maria had an accident at the ice rink and banged her head on the ice. She had taken some children skating in her capacity as a teacher. She said that one of the boys had bumped into her, on purpose, making her fall backwards and bang her head. She had gone to hospital, but they had said she was all right and could go home. She came straight to the session after that. During the following year this accident and the damage it did to her body became central to her analysis. She experienced a range of physical pains and related them to the accident. The other important theme was her rage with various people, from her GP to the "head" at her school. Although she had expressed such rage before, it was now intensified and felt almost uncontainable in the sessions. Her repetitiveness was also relentless. My patient's sense of being misunderstood and not heard was profound. She indeed felt that a block of cement had hit her and her only way of showing me how she felt was to "hit" me with it as well.

A year after the ice rink accident and two years after starting analysis, Maria was involved in a car crash in which a car came out of a side road and hit hers. She got out of her car and banged on the other driver's window, screaming and shouting, out of control in her fear and fury. She felt that the other driver and the passenger were laughing at her, while people gathered around to watch. She told me that her car was a "write off ".

My hypothesis throughout her analysis had been that these accidents functioned like a screen onto which Maria projected her own, condensed version of her history, already contained in the dream she had told me at the beginning of her analysis. The analysis has attempted to recover the unconscious processes, which these accidents may both express and mask, and so introduce a difference in Maria's way of experiencing herself and others.

The analytic task involved expanding the chains of associations, which place the various phenomena in the context in which they occurred. This also implies that, for a long time, the emphasis of the analysis was on the form and *functions* of the patient's communications rather than on the content of the material.

Maria feared that to experience herself in relation to me was to become imprisoned in a violent world and to succumb to what she experienced as my wish to take her over and tear her to pieces. In this context, she could not have a mind of her own because she feared my thoughts about her and their potential malignancy and destructiveness towards her. She could only find in the other, repetitions of herself and of her internal objects. The dilemmas for the transference are obvious, and she attempted to deal with her terror of me by carefully watching and regulating how much she could actually interact with me at each session. If there was an obvious sadomasochism implied in her frequent lateness to the sessions, and in the process of relentlessly telling me about the minutiae of the functioning of her body, I felt that the main function of all this was not to attack me, but to defend her very survival.

The dream about the block of cement has been understood by both of us as encapsulating most of the story of her analysis and her experience of it. Both of us were trapped by a block of cement in a two-dimensional world, unable to feel or think, running around like cartoon characters. The analytical task consisted of introducing differences into this two-dimensional world.

Michael, a recurrent dream and its transformation

Michael had a recurrent dream since childhood:

There was a big white screen in front of him. Suddenly a black animal appeared and rushed through the bottom of the screen, or some kind of black spot ran through and corroded the screen.

This dream used to terrify him. He remembers having it whilst in hospital after an operation. It made him feel sick then and he still feels ill when he has the dream, although this is now rare. In the course of the analysis we were able to understand some of the meaning of this dream, although the greatest insight was reached after an event in a session, that brought this dream dramatically to the transference.

Michael was a young, German man who came to analysis after a serious suicide attempt that led to hospitalization. He was born blind and remained blind for the first couple of years of his life. A series of operations then allowed him to gain sight.

One of Michael's first statements in the very first session of his analysis was about his experience that throughout his life he had been talking to a voice in his head, and that now he was actually talking to a voice behind him. He felt as if my voice had always existed, but had now become real. This communication pointed to the idealization with which he started his relationship with me. I already had a place in his mind; indeed, I had been there for a long time.

There was, however, also another side to this coin. Michael brought another dream to his first session; a dream that he felt was one of the most disturbing he had ever had.

He was in a room, and in this room he was God. There had been a car accident and there was a baby's cot. As God he had the power to decide whether this baby was going to live or to die. He decided that the baby should live. Then the whole thing repeated itself in a circle like a loop and he was at the top looking at everything happening and again he was in a position to decide whether the child was going to live or to die. In the end he decided that the child would die.

He woke up in the middle of that and felt really frightened and wanted to go back to the dream in order to make the child live.

In that session I talked to him about the two impossible positions contained in the dream. In one he was God, with powers of life and death over another part of him that he experienced as a helpless baby. In the other *he* was a helpless baby, whose fate was in the hands of somebody all-powerful. I thought that he feared that this was all he could expect from analysis. I, too, could only be in one of these positions, as God, or a helpless baby who would meet my fate at his hand. He was terrified of what we could do to each other. The inevitability of death was there at the outset, in this narrative.

During the initial months, the right amount of contact was essential in our sessions: if I said too little, Michael would become quiet and withdrawn, almost lifeless; if I said too much, he felt too intruded upon and disorganized. The dance between us required a certain rhythm whereby we were intensely involved with each other, and this evoked in me thoughts about a rhythm that should have been present in his interactions with his mother as a small child. What I have in mind is related to Stern's notion of the ways in which mothers "tune in" to their babies. This was a relationship where mother and baby could not hold each other with their eyes and where bodily and sound contact appeared to me to have been intense.

Other temporal dimensions slowly emerged in Michael's material. In adolescence his mind was filled with conscious fantasies of violence and in young adulthood he engaged in violent relationships with his girlfriends and peers. Through violence, he attempted to exercise mastery over a world that was experienced as frightening and senseless. Some months into the analysis I began to realize that, for Michael, in the transference, there was also an enormous confusion between intimacy and sexuality. He alternated between omnipotent phantasies of having seduced me into being his analyst on the one hand and the terror of abandonment on the other. Different time dimensions could be comprehended in these experiences: the terrorized infant being cared for by a mother he could not see but only feel and hear, and the advent of genital sexuality that was superimposed over that more primitive material.

The beginnings of Michael's analysis were characterized by his wish to control me and the demand that I should provide him with clear structures so that he would be able to see where he was. In a concrete way he used to write my interpretations down and spread them around his flat over the weekends. His fear was that of fragmentation and psychotic breakdown. He was terrified of dependence, as it brought with it the panic he had experienced in the past in relation to his mother's inability to contain his terror and preventing terrible things happening to him (images and memories of being taken away from her to undergo an eye operation).

Michael's first year of analysis was characterized by a paradox. He was compelled to attack the things which were important to him. Thus, the more Michael felt attached to his analyst; the more dangerous it was for both of us. Michael became able to acknowledge his terror that I would derive pleasure from hurting him or humiliating him, especially if I knew of his need for me. This was an expression of himself as he could only find in the outside world repetitions of himself.

In one session, a few weeks before the first summer break, I felt that he was terrified of his experience that I was important to him and said so to him. He responded by quoting "The man had killed the thing he loved ...".[1] This was accompanied by a chilling feeling I had in the counter-transference. I briefly felt invaded by an intense, inexplicable fear. There was a long, heavy silence, which Michael finally interrupted by saying that he had had a strange feeling that his jaws were dry. This was the feeling that tended to accompany the dream of the white screen, which was being corroded, damaged. He had not had the feeling for quite some time and had even forgotten that the dream was accompanied by such a feeling. The experience of the real potential for damage, murder, and suicide had come fully into the transference. This session had taken place before a holiday break and at a different level we were confronting the experience of impending blackness on the eve of a separation that left him in the dark. I put this interpretation to him.

At the following session, Michael brought the following dream:

He went into a building, where there was a library with books. It was inside a Victorian museum about murder. There was a man, a doctor, who was going to perform an operation on a woman with a broken leg. The operation lasted fifty minutes, during which time he killed her. He then replaced her with another woman, also with a broken leg, so that no one would suspect what had happened. There were, however, enough clues for someone using modern investigation methods to find out about what had happened. My patient was watching the scene and tried to escape. He ran to another floor. He kept trying to escape, running away and then he woke up.

I cannot, within the limits of this chapter, give a full account of this session. As Michael told me the dream, I immediately remembered the fear that had invaded me at the previous session, and thought that he was about to stop the analysis out of his fear of himself and me. However, what struck me most during his account of the dream was the slow, monotonous, almost hypnotic quality of his narrative, which contrasted both with the frightening content of the dream, as well as the usual intense quality of our interaction in the sessions. I waited, and after a while, Michael carried on giving further and further details about the dream, describing the glass windows, and the bookcases in the library, away from the central events in the dream. I commented on my sense of his detachment from the dream during the session, and he agreed, although he had woken up terrorized. This detached quality had also been underlined in the content of the dream itself (for example, he had been an observer of the events, and they had taken place in a museum). I told Michael that I felt that this dream had been too frightening for him, and that he could not relate to it. He seemed to understand both this, and the idea that his terror of the damage he felt that we could do to each other was now also present in the session.

The dream narrated a primal scene between a castrated, damaged, woman, who was also ultimately a fake, because she was just a replacement for another, dead woman, and a murderer. This encounter was experienced by Michael as what took place in the sessions, between us. In the dream the patient ran away, although a positive aspect of the dream could be found in the idea that there were enough clues for a modern investigation to find out what had really happened, i.e. to discover that murder and castration had taken place. Over some of the sessions that followed this dream Michael's dilemma became apparent: he was frightened that the only way of avoiding damage might be to run away, and therefore kill off the analysis.

The work we did on this dream and its underlying anxieties did not prevent Michael from leaving the analysis. He did not come his sessions in the following week, the last week before the summer break. I wrote to him, saying that I understood his reasons for feeling he needed to stay away, but that I was keeping his sessions open to him until a week after the end of the summer break.

Michael came back after the summer, and we were able to carry on working for another few years. As the analysis progressed life became a bit more ordinary. Michael once remembered how, as a child, whenever he hurt himself, there was a panic that something serious had happened. He was able to remember situations when friends of his would get hurt, but did not necessarily run home to disinfect the wound. One friend, after scratching himself while playing football once said to him, in reply to his concern: "Don't worry, it's nothing". He then said to me: "I could not believe that he didn't think straight away that his arm was going to get infected, turn green and fall off". Whenever Michael felt that there was a scratch between us, his fear was that everything was going to turn terribly wrong.

In the first few years, therefore, analysis was marked by the possibility of damage between us in terms of psychotic breakdown or accidents, especially at weekends and holiday breaks. Progressively this was understood and inserted into the language of the transference, and words gradually became mediators for actions. Dreams became a language through which to express the relationship of the transference. I think that there is an isomorphism between some of the dreams that Michael brought to analysis. The initial dream of "the killer god and the baby", was already a transformation of the "dream of the white screen". A year into analysis, the dream of "the museum of murder", brought the issues crucially to the transference. This dream was concretely experienced as a source of danger, leading to a breakdown in the analysis from which we were able to recover.

In a session nearly a year after the dream of "the museum of murder" Michael had a dream that

he was going to be fired because he belonged to an anarchistic organization called "Chateaubriand".

The associations to Chateaubriand led to thoughts about luxury and abundance, a delicious meal that he could now associate with analysis and coming to see me. He thought I was French, because of my accent, my French car and also a French book he had seen in my consulting room. He experienced me as introducing anarchy, desire into a world that had previously been experienced as fundamentally bureaucratic and dictatorial.

Michael's treatment was successful and it allowed him to build a relationship with a woman and a deeper understanding of himself. Towards the end of it he often commented on how much he had changed and how much more he could see and understand about himself.

The theme of the dream screen was progressively experienced in the transference. Throughout his analysis, we progressively understood some of the layers of this dream, which was over-determined; his experience of destroying the ecstatic idealized union with the white screen, the maternal breasts. In his analysis, he was frightened that I would not be able to cope with what he regarded as his cruelty, nastiness, and mess. We also understood his need for idealized images of his objects, as extensions of his wishes. His attacks became ways of punishing his objects, so that they would change into what he wanted them to be. This could easily be reversed into an attack on himself.

Michael did not attempt suicide after the beginning of his analysis. Towards the end of his analysis Michael started a relationship with a girlfriend and felt more in control of his life. The changes in him could well be mapped in the changes of the quality and narrative of his dreams.

Robert and the house surrounded by glass

Robert's first contact with me was via a letter, telling me the story of his life. He enclosed with this same letter a self-portrait, painted many years earlier. Being a painter, he had felt unable to paint during the previous ten years. He came from an artistic, upper middle class Italian family, with eight children, from whom he had taken flight. His father and sister were successful artists. His mother had also been successful, prior to a series of psychotic breakdowns, which had caused her to be hospitalized several times. In reading this well-written and engrossing letter, I already had an inkling of a position he wanted to keep me in: it was not a story that he told in my presence, which might have allowed some exchanges between us. I was to read what he had written, outside an actual interaction between us.

Robert then phoned me and we arranged an initial consultation. A handsome man in his early thirties, Robert entered the room, full of seductive sexual vitality, but also barely able to disguise his fear of me. I had the immediate thought that he felt confused about this encounter and that he might experience it as a scene of seduction. Indeed, for the first half of the session Robert proceeded to tell me about his intense affairs with older women, that he had only managed to sustain for brief periods of time. I thought that it was important to address his confusion at the outset, and immediately let him know that I thought that he was confused about what I expected from him. He calmed down visibly, relaxing back in the chair, and was then able to tell me about his great pain at not being able to paint for such a long time, and the life full of violent encounters that he had led since he had stopped painting.

At the end of that first consultation he wanted to start analysis with me, and we began the following week. At his first session, he brought me the following dream:

There was a beautiful house, the most beautiful house one could imagine, surrounded by lush gardens, and filled with works of art and famous paintings. It was very spacious, one room leading to another. There was glass surrounding it, however, and one was not able to penetrate it. One had to admire it from the outside.

This dream and the associations, which proceeded and followed it, became paradigmatic of the many layers of Robert's analysis. My experience of his letter immediately came to mind, his wish to be admired like this beautiful house filled with works of art, which left himself, as well as the other, on the outside. There was no live communication between inside and outside, and between his inner world and the external. Everything was either locked in or out. This was a dream we repeatedly came back to during our work together. The house also represented the body of a mother whom he experienced as ungiving and impenetrable. Finally, it represented his fear that whatever he produced would be trapped inside her. It was his terror of what the body and the mind of his psychotic mother contained that constituted the core of what we were to explore in his analysis.

Robert's first dream provided a map to which we turned to understand a great deal about the unfolding of the analytic relationship during the first two years of our work together. Robert's implicit demand was that I should admire him, without attempting to enter into too much contact with him. He came to the sessions full of vivid dreams and thoughts, associations, and interpretations about them. He worked very hard himself both in the sessions and outside them, on his many thoughts, experiences, and impressions. His fundamental requirement was that I should simply admire him and his work, without intervening. I was left outside the house. The interesting point of technique for me in my work with Robert that I would like to indicate, is that this is what I fundamentally did for quite some time, aware that I was doing so. My interpretations and comments, especially at the beginning, were indeed sparse although I felt intensely present with him in the sessions. I was aware that interaction was unbearable to him. Slowly, Robert's fear of relating to me shifted and it was possible to have a different way of interacting with him in the sessions, a sense of a dialogue that could more easily be put into words that he could tolerate.

Some two years after the beginning of his analysis, Robert started painting again. The conflict he had been struggling with was given vivid expression when he wanted to give me the first painting he was able to paint after such a long time. My refusal to accept it and his utter surprise allowed him to believe fully, perhaps for the first time, that our work together was fundamentally for his benefit. He started to participate in exhibitions and competitions, and won a prestigious prize in Italy. The quality of his dreams progressively changed.

In one of the last dreams he brought:

he was in the kitchen cooking with his girlfriend, and they went for a long walk in a beautiful garden, full of rare and exotic flowers.

At that time, Robert had a relationship with a girlfriend and had been offered work teaching art in a small town in Italy, which was going to give him time to develop his own painting. His girlfriend went with him. Some aspect of the relationship with me was still idealized, but as he left there was a sense that he would be able to carry on the work we had started.

The tradition of dreams as oracles

In his monumental review of existing theories on dreams, Freud distinguished between those authors who thought that only the trivial is expressed in dreams, those who viewed dreams as somatic experiences, and yet others who thought that it is only that which is not dealt with that is presented in dreams. Already, in 1891, Delae suggested that dreams were unrecognized reproductions (*souvenir inconscient*) of material already experienced (in Freud, 1900, p. 81). By naming his work *The Interpretation of Dreams*, Freud was joining a long tradition that emphasized the intrinsic value of dreams and their *interpretation*.

In surveying the scientific literature on dreams, Freud remarked on the attitude toward dreams which prevailed during classical antiquity: "They took it as axiomatic that dreams were connected with the world of superhuman beings in whom they believed and that they were revelations from gods and daemons" (Lorand, 1955).

The ideas that oracles predicted the future and that the future was often expressed in dreams are not new. In classical Greece, Isis, Osiris, and Serapis delivered their oracles by means of dreams (see Devereux, 1976). Socrates thought of dreams as originating from the gods, and thus ascribed a prophetic meaning to them. In referring to the Hebrew sources of dream interpretations, Freud mentions the biblical dream of Joseph.

In general, ancient peoples believed that dreams were sent by the gods to guide human beings in their decisions and actions. Moreover, they regarded dreams as either favourable or hostile manifestations. This belief was held by the Phoenicians, Egyptians, and especially by the Babylonians, with whom the Hebrews had much contact and from whose culture they borrowed extensively.

Breton suggested that Freud had been mistaken in not believing in the prophetic nature of dreams, and their engagement with the immediate future, when he emphasized dreams as revealing the past. As a consequence he denied dreams the quality of movement (1938). The question of prophetic dreams was a matter for scientific debate throughout the nineteenth century, and was discussed by philosophers such as Shopenhauer, Vashide, and Pieron.

On the atemporality of dreams: the repetition compulsion

The association between dreams and earlier experiences, between the present and the past lies at the core of Freud's thinking about dreams (see also Anzieu, 1986; Sharpe, 1937):

On this view a dream might be described *as a substitute for an infantile scene modified by being transferred onto a recent experience.* The infantile scene is unable to bring about its own revival and has to be content with returning as a dream. [*S.E..*, *V*, p. 546]

Dreaming, he adds later " is a piece of infantile life that has been superseded (p. 567).

The connections between the present and the past are thus established and understood. But what about the future?

The notion of the compulsion to repeat was to be developed many years after he wrote *The Interpretation of Dreams.* In 1909, however, when discussing the case of Little Hans, Freud had already proposed: "... a thing which has not been understood inevitably reappears; like an unlaid ghost, it cannot rest until the mystery has been solved and the spell broken" (1909, p. 122). The notion of repetition compulsion was further discussed in *Remembering, Repeating and Working through* (1914). To my mind, these ideas open the way for us to understand not only repetitive dreams—like Michael's dream from childhood—but also patterns one can identify in the dreams of most patients. That which has not been understood or worked through is repeated in dreams. In the dreams, which are dreamt for the analyst in an analysis, patients are also bringing that which they want to work on in the analysis, so that these experiences are not repeated, unmodified, into the future.[2]

Maria brings her experience of the loss of her three-dimensionality, and repeats in the transference a relationship with a dead mother "who is not there" available to think about her little girl. Robert brings the experience of his internal space with which he cannot communicate, in relation to which he either feels excluded or locked in. His dilemma is between his desire for creative work, on the one hand, and his terror of feeling trapped in the unimaginable relationship with a psychotic mother, on the other. Represented in his initial dream is his inability to be in contact with himself and his desires. Michael's dream expresses the terror of his aggression and fear of the damage that can take place between people.

Pontalis has suggested that "the dream is what makes things visible, what gives its visible place to déjà vu, which has become invisible" (1974).

An important aspect of the sequence narrated in Michael's analysis, lies in the fact that an experience in the consulting room (the dry jaw, his fear, and mine) followed by an interpretation, allowed a dream to be dreamt. Money-Kyrle has suggested a theory of stages in representational thought that goes from a stage of concrete representation (where no distinction is made between the representation and the object represented), through ideographic representation, as in dreams, to a stage of conscious and predominantly verbal thought (1968, p. 422). I think that in Michael's case the experience in the consulting room, which included the analyst's counter-transference, took place before it could be represented in dreams. The interpretations function as mediator in this process. This observation is in agreement with Sedlack's (this book) observation on the analyst's function in the transformation of patients' dilemmas into ones that can be thought and dreamt about. In his paper Sedlack also addresses the role of the counter-transference in the process.

Pontalis has suggested that to Freud dreams represented a displaced maternal body, and in interpreting dreams Freud commits incest with the body of his dreams, penetrating their secrets. In the process, Freud emerged as Oedipus (1974, p. 26).

> My hypothesis is that every dream, as an object in analysis, refers to the maternal body ... It is not the dream's contents, but the subject's "use" of it that reveals his true pathology. The dream-object is caught up secondarily in an oral, anal, phallic organisation, but the dream process is originally linked to the mother: the variety of scripts represented in it, and even the range of meanings he invests in the therapy (faeces, present, work of art, "imaginary child", hidden treasure, "interesting organ", fetish) unfold against the background of this exclusive relationship. Dreaming is above all the attempt to maintain an impossible union with the mother, to preserve an undivided whole, *to move in a space prior to time*. This is why some patients implicitly ask one not to get too close to their dreams, neither to touch nor to manipulate the body of the dream, not to change the "thing presentation" to a "verbal presentation". [p. 29]

In dreaming, therefore, one is effecting this eternal return to the primitive relationship with the mother. The incest prohibition is characterized by Freud as perhaps the "most maiming wound ever inflicted ... on the erotic life of man" (Freud, 1930, p. 74). "We are fighting this war", Aureliano José is told, in *A Hundred years of Solitude*, "so that a person can marry his own mother" (Garcia Marquez, 1998, p. 127).

In a letter to Fliess Freud stated:

I have found love of the mother and jealousy of the father in my
own case too, and now believe it to be a general phenomenon of
early childhood ... The Greek myth seizes on a compulsion which
everyone recognizes because he has felt traces of it in himself. [15
October 1897, F/F 272]

At the end of Chapter VII, Freud asks, "And the value of dreams
for giving us knowledge of the future?" He answers his question
thus: "There is of course no question of that. It would be truer to say
instead that they give us knowledge of the past" (1900. p. 621).

Dreams that bring knowledge of the past in his formulation may
also be interpreted as foretelling the future. Freud himself continues:

Nevertheless the ancient belief that dreams foretell the future is not
wholly devoid of truth. By picturing our wishes as fulfilled, dreams
are after all leading us into the future. But this future, which the
dreamer pictures as the present, has been moulded by his
indestructible wish into a perfect likeness of the past. [ibid.]

In the patients I discussed in this chapter, the body of the
mother, as expressed in their dreams and the beginnings of their
analysis, was not experienced as a home, a safe place that allowed
for exploration and creativity. In each of their analysis there was a
search for a mental space where they could explore, think about,
and transform the relationships with their internal objects.

Notes

1. "in the ballad of Reading Jail" (Poem by Oscar Wilde).
2. Ferenczi thought of repetitive dreams as the oneiric compulsive
   repetition of a traumatic event.

References

Anzieu, D. (1986) Freud's Self Analysis. New York: International
    Universities Press.
Beratis, S. (1984). The first analytic dream: mirror of the patient's

neurotic conflicts and subsequent analytic process. *International Journal of Psycho-Analysis, 65*: 461–469.

Bressler, B. (1961). First dream in analysis. Their relationship to early memories and the pre-oedipal mother. *Psychoanalysis & Psychoanalytical Review, 48*(4): 60–82.

Breton, A. (1938). *Trajectoire du Revè*. Paris: Editions G.L.M.

Devereux, G. (1976). *Dreams in Greek Tragedy*. Berkeley and Los Angeles: University of California Press.

Freud, S. (1900). *The Interpretation of Dreams. S.E.*, 4 and 5.

Freud, S. (1909). Analysis of a phobia in a five year old boy. *S.E., 10*.

Freud, S. (1914). Remembering, repeating and working through. *S.E., 12*.

Freud, S. (1915). *Mourning and Melancholia. S.E., 14*.

Freud, S. (1920). Beyond the pleasure principle. *S.E., 18*.

Freud, S. (1924). The economic problem of masochism. *S.E., 19*.

Freud, S. (1937a). Analysis terminable and interminable. *S.E., 23*.

Freud, S. (1941 [1921]). Psychoanalysis and telepathy. *S.E., 28*: 177–194.

Freud, S. (1922). Dreams and telepathy. *S.E., 28*: 195–200.

Freud, S. (1930[1929]). *Civilization and its Discontents. S.E., 21*.

Flanders, S. (1993). *The Dream Discourse Today*. London: Routledge and The Institute of Psycho-Analysis.

Franco, D., & Levine, A. (1969). Psychic reality and psychic structure as predicted from the manifest content of first dreams. *Proceedings 77th Annual Convention, APA*, pp. 4593–4594.

Garcia Marquez, G. (1998). *One Hundred Years of Solitude*. Harmondsworth: Essential Penguin.

Green, A. (1993). *Le Travail du Negatif*. Paris: Les Editions de Minuit.

Greenacre, P. (1975). On reconstruction. *Journal of the American Psychoanalytical Association, 23*: 693–712.

Khan, M. Masud (1972). The use and abuse of dream in psychic experience. *International Journal of Psychoanalytic Psychotherapy, 1* [also in Flanders, S. (Ed.) (1993). *The Dream Discourse Today*].

Lewin, B. (1946). Sleep, mouth and the dream screen. *Psychoanalytic Quarterly, 15*: 419–434.

Lewin, B. (1948). Inferences from the Dream Screen. *International Journal of Psycho-Analysis, 29*: 224–231.

Lorand, S. (1955). Dream interpretation in The Talmud. *International Journal of Psycho-Analysis, 38*: 92–97.

Marcus, L. (Ed.) (1999). *Sigmund Freud's The Interpretation of Dreams: New Interdisciplinary Essays*. Manchester: Manchester University Press.

Money-Kyrle, R. (1968). Cognitive development. *International Journal of Psycho-Analysis, 49* [also in Meltzer, D. (Ed.) *The Collected Papers of Roger Money-Kyrle.* Perthshire: Clunie Press, 1978].

Pontalis, J.-B. (1974). Dream as an object. *International Review of Psychoanalysis, 1* [also in *Frontiers in Psychoanalysis: Between the Dream and Psychic Pain.* London: The Hogarth Press and The Institute of Psycho-Analysis, 1981].

Sandler, J., & Sandler, A-M. (1994). The past unconscious and the present unconscious: a contribution to a technical frame of reference. *Psychoanalytic Study of the Child, 49:* 278–291.

Sharpe, E. F. (1937). *Dream Analysis.* London: The Hogarth Press.

Segal, H. (1986). The function of dreams. In: *The Work of Hanna Segal* [also in Flanders, S. (Ed.) (1993) *The Dream Discourse Today*].

Stekel, W. (1943). *The Interpretation of Dreams.* New York: Liveright Publishing Corporation.

Stewart, H. (1973). The experience of the dream and the transference. *International Journal of Psycho-Analysis, 54* [also in Flanders, S. (Ed.) (1993). *The Dream Discourse Today*].

INDEX